LEARN TO

Quilt Table Runners & Placemats

Stepping Stones, page 42

www.companyscoming.com
visit our website

Land & Sea Bargello Placemats, page 22

Learn to Quilt Table Runners & Placemats

Copyright © Company's Coming Publishing Limited

All rights reserved worldwide. No part of this book may be reproduced, stored in a retrieval system or transmitted in any form by any means without permission in advance from the publisher.

In the case of photocopying or other reprographic copying, a license may be purchased from the Canadian Copyright Licensing Agency (Access Copyright). Visit www.accesscopyright.ca or call 1-800-893-5777. In the United States, please contact the Copyright Clearance Centre, www.copyright.com or call 978-750-8400.

Brief portions of this book may be reproduced for review purposes, provided credit is given to the source. Reviewers are invited to contact the publisher for additional information.

The contents of this publication were provided especially for Company's Coming Publishing Limited under an exclusive license agreement with the copyright owner, DRG Texas, LP ("DRG"). The contents are not available for commercial use or sale outside of this publication, but are intended only for personal use. Every effort has been made to ensure that the instructions in this publication are complete and accurate; however, neither DRG nor Company's Coming Publishing Limited can be held responsible for any human error, typographical mistake or variation in the results achieved by the user.

First Printing April 2012

Library and Archives Canada Cataloguing in Publication
Learn to quilt table runners & placemats.
(Workshop series)
Includes index.
ISBN 978-1-897477-77-9
1. Quilting. 2. Runners (Household linens). 3. Place mats. I. Title: Quilt table runners & placemats.
II. Title: Quilt table runners and placemats. III. Series: Workshop series (Edmonton, Alta.)
TT835.L375 2012   746.46   C2011-906145-7

Published by
Company's Coming Publishing Limited
2311-96 Street
Edmonton, Alberta, Canada T6N 1G3
Tel: 780-450-6223   Fax: 780-450-1857
www.companyscoming.com

Printed in China

The Company's Coming Story

Jean Paré grew up with an understanding that family, friends and home cooking are the key ingredients for a good life. A mother of four, Jean worked as a professional caterer for 18 years, operating out of her home kitchen. During that time, she came to appreciate quick and easy recipes that call for everyday ingredients. In answer to mounting requests for her recipes, Company's Coming cookbooks were born, and Jean moved on to a new chapter in her career.

In the beginning, Jean worked from a spare bedroom in her home, located in the small prairie town of Vermilion, Alberta, Canada. The first Company's Coming cookbook, *150 Delicious Squares*, was an immediate bestseller. Today, with well over 150 titles in print, Company's Coming has earned the distinction of publishing Canada's most popular cookbooks. The company continues to gain new supporters by adhering to Jean's "Golden Rule of Cooking"—Never share a recipe you wouldn't use yourself. It's an approach that has worked—millions of times over!

Company's Coming cookbooks are distributed throughout Canada, the United States, Australia and other international English-language markets. French and Spanish language editions have also been published. Sales to date have surpassed 30 million copies with no end in sight. Familiar and trusted in home kitchens around the world, Company's Coming cookbooks are highly regarded both as kitchen workbooks and as family heirlooms.

Company's Coming founder Jean Paré

Just as Company's Coming continues to promote the tradition of home cooking, the same is now true with crafting. Like good cooking, great craft results depend upon easy-to-follow instructions, readily available materials and enticing photographs of the finished products. Also like cooking, crafting is meant to be enjoyed in the home or cottage. Company's Coming Crafts, then, is a natural extension from the kitchen into the family room or den.

Because Company's Coming operates a test kitchen and not a craft shop, we've partnered with a major North American craft content publisher to assemble a variety of craft compilations exclusively for us. Our editors have been involved every step of the way. You can see the excellent results for yourself in the book you're holding.

Company's Coming Crafts are for everyone—whether you're a beginner or a seasoned pro. What better gift could you offer than something you've made yourself? In these hectic days, people still enjoy crafting parties; they bring family and friends together in the same way a good meal does. Company's Coming is proud to support crafters with this new creative book series.

We hope you enjoy these easy-to-follow, informative and colourful books, and that they inspire your creativity. So, don't delay—get crafty!

TABLE OF CONTENTS

Foreword 7 • Quilt-Making Basics 8

Summerset Kitchen Collection, page 18

Lollipop Spring, page 26

Charmed Runner & Coasters, page 62

Country Garden, page 58

TABLE OF CONTENTS

Throughout the Year

Add seasonal ambiance with these festive placemats and table runners.

When Elegance Is the Answer

Create a beautiful table for those special occasions.

Pleasingly Paisley Table Topper, page 118

Hooray for Holidays, page 76

Blue Sky Autumn, page 90

Four-Panel Table Runner, page 100

Make it yourself!

CRAFT WORKSHOP SERIES

Get a craft class in a book! General instructions teach basic skills or how to apply them in a new way. Easy-to-follow steps, diagrams and photos make projects simple.

Whether paper crafting, knitting, crocheting, beading, sewing or quilting—find beautiful, fun designs you can make yourself.

COLLECT THEM ALL!

Kids Learn To Knit, Quilt And Crochet
Learn To Bead Earrings
Learn To Bead Jewellery
Learn To Craft With Paper
Learn To Crochet For Baby
Learn To Crochet In A Day
Learn To Knit For Baby
Learn To Knit In The Round
Learn To Knit Socks
Learn To Make Cards With Folds
Learn To Make Cards With Photos
Learn To Quilt Fat Quarters
Learn To Quilt With Panels
Learn To Sew For The Table

FOREWORD

A beautiful table sets the mood or tone for any gathering, whether it is an intimate dinner with friends, a casual open house or a more formal gathering. Table runners and placemats can be used everyday or for special events, parties and holidays. No matter what the occasion, a pretty table adds to your decor.

Warm weather invites outdoor dining, cookouts and more festive, fun events! Bright fabric choices combined with interesting patterns flood your table with colour. Whether you enjoy working with precut fabric, doing appliqué or just mixing and matching your most colourful fat quarters, you will find a pattern that fits your needs in the first chapter.

If a more traditional quilting pattern suits the occasion, the second chapter offers several choices. Different shapes and piecing techniques add dimension to the various table runners and placemats that can be used on buffets or end tables as well as dining tables. Change up the fabrics and come up with your own unique look!

The third chapter takes you through the year's cooler seasons and holidays starting with Christmas, winter and Valentine's Day and ending with the beautiful colours of fall. Log Cabin blocks, appliqué and pieced quilts make up a beautiful selection of patterns for those special days throughout the year.

More formal looks complete the selection of table runners and placemats in the final chapter. Different shapes and matching sets are represented for those occasions that require a more elegant presentation. Paisleys and floral fabrics are perfect for most of these patterns. Or try a more contemporary look with the black-and-white prints and red accents that are used in It Hits the Spot Runner.

Table runners and placemats are fun quilting projects that many times can be completed in an evening. Most patterns represented in this book are beginner patterns, with an intermediate pattern added to enhance your skills. Full-colour photos and clearly written instructions make it easy to create all these great items, so get out your stash and start quilting!

Summer Picnic Placemats, page 68

QUILT-MAKING BASICS

Materials & Supplies

Fat Quarter Fabrics

A fat quarter is fabric yardage cut half the fabric-width by half a yard—in most fabrics this size is 22" x 18". For some projects, this size works better than a regular quarter-yard of fabric that would be 9" by the width of the fabric, usually 42"–45".

Some projects require pieces larger than 9" for appliqué shapes or corner triangles. These larger shapes cannot be cut from a quarter-yard of fabric, but can be cut from fat quarters.

Most fabric stores will not custom-cut fat quarters, but they do sell them. They choose which fabrics they want to cut up for this purpose. In some stores, just one fat quarter is available, while in other stores coordinated sets of fabric are selected and bundled in an attractive way to show off the colours. These bundles are hard to resist!

If you like to have lots of different fabrics available whenever you start to sew, collect fat quarters in a variety of colours and prints, and get ready to have some fun.

Thread

For most piecing, good-quality cotton or cotton-covered polyester is the thread of choice. Inexpensive polyester threads are not recommended because they can cut the fibres of cotton fabrics.

Choose a colour of thread that will match or blend with the fabrics in your quilt. For projects pieced with dark- and light-coloured fabrics, choose a neutral thread colour, such as a medium grey, as a compromise between colours. Test by pulling a sample seam.

Batting

Batting is the material used to give a quilt loft or thickness. It also adds warmth.

Some qualities to look for in batting are drapeability, resistance to fibre migration, loft and softness.

Tools & Equipment

There are few truly essential tools and little equipment required for quilt making. Basics include needles (hand-sewing and betweens), pins (long, thin, sharp pins are best), sharp scissors or shears, a thimble, template materials (plastic or cardboard), marking tools (chalk markers, water-erasable pens and a No. 2 pencil are a few) and a quilting frame or hoop. For piecing and/or quilting by machine, add a sewing machine to the list.

Other sewing basics are also necessary, such as a seam ripper, pincushion, measuring tape and an iron. For making strip-pieced quilts, a rotary cutter, rotary cutting mat and specialty rulers are essential.

Construction Methods

Traditional Templates

There are two types—templates that include a ¼" seam allowance and those that don't.

Choose the template material and the pattern. Transfer the pattern shapes to the template material with a sharp No. 2 pencil. Write the pattern name, piece letter or number, grain line and number to cut for one block or whole quilt on each piece as shown in Figure 1.

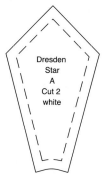

Figure 1

Some patterns require a reversed piece (Figure 2). These patterns are labelled with an R after the piece letter; for example, B and BR. To reverse a template, first cut it with the labelled side up and then with the labelled side down. Or, place two layers of fabric with right sides together and cut two pieces at once; one will be reversed.

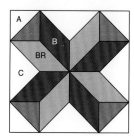

Figure 2

Machine-Piecing

If making templates, include the ¼" seam allowance on the template for machine-piecing. Place template on the wrong side of the fabric as for hand-piecing, except butt pieces against one another when tracing.

Set machine on 2.5 or 12–15 stitches per 1". Join pieces as for hand-piecing, beginning and ending sewing at the end of the fabric patch. No backstitching is necessary when machine-stitching.

Quick-Cutting

Templates can be completely eliminated when using a rotary cutter with a plastic ruler and mat to cut fabric strips.

Always cut away from your body, holding the ruler firmly with the non-cutting hand.

Cutting Strips

Iron fabric to remove wrinkles. Fold in half lengthwise, bringing selvages together. Fold in half again (Figure 3). Be sure there aren't any wrinkles in the fabric.

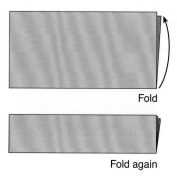

Fold

Fold again

Figure 3

Square-up the fabric first: place folded fabric on cutting mat with the fabric length on the right, or on the left for left-handed cutters (Figure 4). Line up the fold of fabric along one of the mat grid lines.

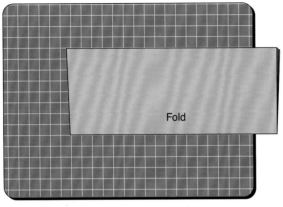

Right-handed

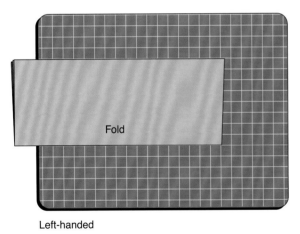

Left-handed

Figure 4

Place acrylic ruler near cut edge, with ruler markings even with mat grid. Hold ruler firmly with left hand (right hand for left-handers), with small finger off the mat to provide extra stability. Hold rotary cutter with blade against ruler and cut away from you in one motion (Figure 5).

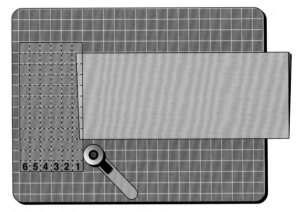

Right-handed

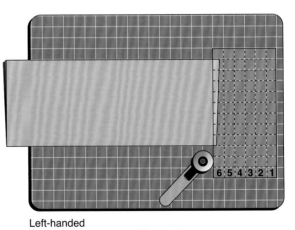

Left-handed

Figure 5

Place ruler with appropriate width line along cut edge of fabric and cut a strip (Figure 6). Continue cutting the number of strips needed for your project.

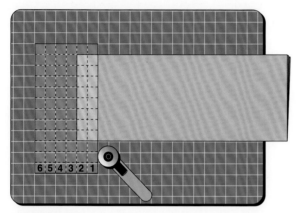

Right-handed

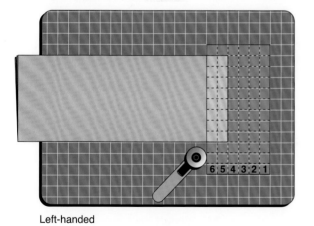

Left-handed

Figure 6

Note: *After cutting a few strips, check to make sure your fabric is squared up and re-square if necessary. If you don't, your strips may have a "v" in the centre (Figure 7), causing inaccurate piecing.*

Figure 7

Quick-Piecing Method

Lay pieces to be joined under the presser foot of the sewing machine with right sides together. Sew an exact ¼" seam allowance to the end of the piece; place another unit right next to the first one and continue sewing, adding a piece after every stitched piece, until all of the pieces are used up (Figure 8).

Figure 8

When sewing is finished, cut the threads that join the pieces apart. Press seam toward the darker fabric.

Appliqué

Making Templates

The appliqué designs given in this book are shown as full-size drawings. The drawings show dotted lines to indicate where one piece overlaps another. Other marks indicate placement of embroidery stitches for decorative purposes such as eyes, lips, flowers, etc.

Before the actual appliqué process begins, cut the background block.

Transfer the design to a large piece of tracing paper. Using a light box, transfer design to fabric background.

If you don't have a light box, tape the pattern on a window; centre the background block on top and tape in place. Trace the design onto the background block with a water-erasable marker, or light lead or chalk pencil. This drawing will mark exactly where the fabric pieces should be placed on the background block.

Hand Appliqué

Traditional hand appliqué uses a template made from the desired finished shape without a seam allowance added.

After the fabric is prepared, trace the desired shape onto the right side of the fabric with a water-erasable marker, or light lead or chalk pencil. Leave at least ½" between design motifs when tracing to allow for the seam allowance when cutting out the shapes.

When the desired number of shapes needed have been drawn on the fabric pieces, cut out shapes, leaving ⅛"–¼" all around drawn lines for turning under.

Turn the shape's edges over on the drawn or stitched line. When turning in concave curves, clip to seam line and fold over the seam allowance as shown in Figure 9; baste in place.

Figure 9

For hand appliqué, position the fabric shapes on the background block and pin or baste them in place. Using a blind stitch or appliqué stitch, sew pieces in place with matching thread and small stitches. Start with background pieces first and work up to foreground pieces.

Machine Appliqué

There are several products available to help make the machine-appliqué process easier and faster.

Fusible transfer web is a commercial product similar to iron-on interfacing except it has two sticky sides. It is used to adhere appliqué shapes to the background with heat. Paper is adhered to one side of the web.

To use, reverse pattern and draw shapes onto the paper side of the web; cut, leaving a margin around each shape. Place on the wrong side of the chosen fabric; fuse in place, referring to the manufacturer's instructions. Cut out shapes on the drawn line. Peel off the paper and fuse in place on the background fabric. Transfer any detail lines to the fabric shapes.

Putting It All Together

Finishing the Top

Settings

Most quilts are made by sewing individual blocks together in rows that, when joined, create a design.

Plain blocks can be alternated with pieced or appliquéd blocks in a straight set (Figure 1).

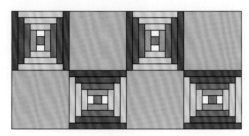

Figure 1

Adding Borders

Borders are an integral part of the quilt and should complement the colours and designs used in the quilt centre.

If fabric strips are added for borders, they may be mitred (Figure 2) or butted (Figure 3) at the corners. To determine the size for butted border strips, measure across the centre of the completed quilt top from one side raw edge to the other side raw edge. This measurement will include a ¼" seam allowance on each side.

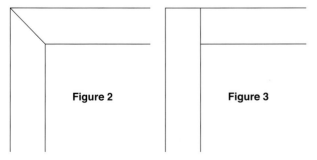

Figure 2   **Figure 3**

Cut two border strips that length by the chosen width of the border. Sew these strips to the top and bottom of the pieced centre, referring to Figure 4. Press the seam allowance toward the border strips.

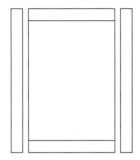

Figure 4

Measure across the completed quilt top at the centre, from top raw edge to bottom raw edge, including the two border strips already added. Cut two border strips that length by the chosen width of the border. Sew a strip to each of the two remaining sides again referring to Figure 4. Press the seams toward the border strips.

To make mitred corners, measure the quilt as before. Add twice the finished width of the border, to allow for mitring, plus ½" for seam allowances to the vertical quilt measurement to determine the length of side border strips. Repeat for horizontal (top and bottom) sides. Sew on each strip, stopping stitching ¼" from corners of centre (Figure 5), leaving the remainder of the strip dangling.

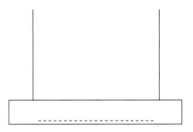

Figure 5

Press corners at a 45-degree angle to form a crease (Figure 6). Stitch from the inside quilt corner to the outside corner on the creased line. Trim excess away after stitching and press mitred seams open (Figure 7).

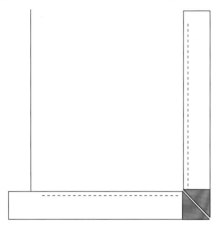

Figure 6

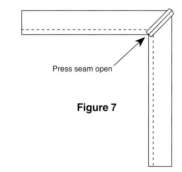

Press seam open

Figure 7

Getting Ready to Quilt

Choosing a Quilting Design

There are several types of quilting designs, some of which do not need to be marked. The easiest of the unmarked designs is in-the-ditch quilting. Here, the quilting stitches are placed in the valley created by the seams joining two pieces together or next to the edge of an appliqué design (Figure 8).

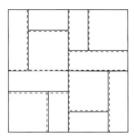

Figure 8

Outline quilting ¼" or more away from seams or appliqué shapes is another no-mark alternative (Figure 9) that prevents having to sew through the layers made by seams, thus making stitching easier.

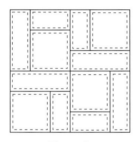

Figure 9

Meander or free-motion quilting by machine fills in open spaces and doesn't require marking. It is fun and easy to stitch as shown in Figure 10.

Figure 10

Marking the Top for Quilting

If you choose a fancy or all-over design for quilting, you will need to transfer the design to your quilt top before layering with the backing and batting. You may use a sharp, medium-lead or silver pencil on light background fabrics. Test the pencil marks to guarantee that they will wash out of your quilt top when quilting is complete, or be sure your quilting stitches cover the pencil marks. Mechanical pencils with very fine points may be used successfully to mark quilts.

Preparing the Quilt Backing

A backing is generally cut at least 4" larger than the quilt top or 2" larger on all sides. For a 64" x 78" finished quilt, the backing would need to be at least 68" x 82".

To avoid having the seam across the centre of the quilt backing, cut or tear one of the right-length pieces in half and sew half to each side of the second piece as shown in Figure 11.

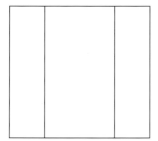

Figure 11

Layering the Quilt Sandwich

Open the batting several days before you need it, to help flatten the creases caused from its being folded up in the bag for so long. Iron the backing piece.

To hold the quilt layers together for quilting, baste by hand or use safety pins. If basting by hand, thread a long thin needle with a long piece of unknotted white or off-white thread. Starting in the centre and leaving a long tail, make 4"–6" stitches toward the outside edge of the quilt top, smoothing as you baste. Start at the centre again and work toward the outside as shown in Figure 12.

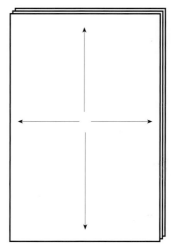

Figure 12

If quilting by machine, you may prefer to use safety pins to hold your fabric sandwich together. Start in the centre of the quilt and pin to the outside, leaving pins open until all are placed. When you are satisfied that all layers are smooth, close the pins.

Quilting

Hand Quilting

To begin, thread a sharp, between needle with an 18" piece of quilting thread. Tie a small knot in the end of the thread. Position the needle about ½" to 1" away from the starting point on quilt top. Sink the needle through the top into the batting layer but not through the backing. Pull the needle up at the starting point of the quilting design. Pull the needle and thread until the knot sinks through the top into the batting (Figure 13).

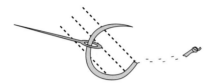

Figure 13

Take small, even running stitches along the marked quilting line. Keep one hand positioned underneath to feel the needle go all the way through to the backing.

When you have nearly run out of thread, wind the thread around the needle several times to make a small knot and pull it close to the fabric. Insert the needle into the fabric on the quilting line and come out with the needle ½" to 1" away, pulling the knot into the fabric layers the same as when you started. Pull and cut thread close to fabric. The end should disappear inside after cutting. Some quilters prefer to take a backstitch with a loop through it for a knot to end.

Machine Quilting

Successful machine quilting requires practice and a good relationship with your sewing machine.

Prepare the quilt for machine quilting in the same way as for hand quilting. Use safety pins to hold the layers together.

Set the machine on a longer stitch length (3.0 or 8–10 stitches per 1") and loosen the amount of pressure on the presser foot. If using marked quilting designs, stitch along the quilting line. An even-feed or walking foot helps to eliminate tucks and puckering by feeding the upper and lower layers through the machine evenly. Special machine-quilting needles work best to penetrate the three layers in your quilt.

Finishing the Edges

To prepare the quilt for the addition of the binding, trim the batting and backing layers flush with the top of the quilt. Using a walking-foot attachment, machine-baste the three layers together all around, approximately ⅛" from the cut edge.

The materials listed for each quilt often include a number of yards of self-made or purchased binding. The advantage of self-made binding is that you can use fabrics from your quilt to coordinate colours.

Double-fold, straight-grain binding is used on projects with right-angle corners. To make this binding, cut 2¼"-wide strips of fabric across the width or down the length of the fabric totalling the perimeter of the quilt plus 10". The strips are joined, as shown in Figure 14, and pressed in half wrong sides together along the length, using an iron on a cotton setting with no steam.

Figure 14

Lining up the raw edges, place the binding on the top of the quilt and begin sewing (again using the walking foot) approximately 6" from the beginning of the binding strip. Stop sewing ¼" from the first corner, leave the needle in the quilt, turn and sew diagonally to the corner as shown in Figure 15.

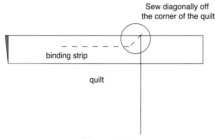

Sew diagonally off
the corner of the quilt

binding strip

quilt

Figure 15

Fold the binding at a 45-degree angle up and away from the quilt as shown in Figure 16 and back down flush with the raw edges. Starting at the top raw edge of the quilt, begin sewing the next side as shown in Figure 17. Repeat at the next three corners.

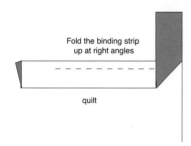

Fold the binding strip
up at right angles

quilt

Figure 16

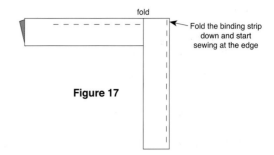

fold

Fold the binding strip
down and start
sewing at the edge

Figure 17

As you approach the beginning of the binding strip, stop stitching and overlap the binding ½" from the edge; trim. Join the two ends with a ¼" seam allowance and press the seam open. Reposition the joined binding along the edge of the quilt and resume stitching to the beginning.

To finish, bring the folded edge of the binding over the raw edges of the quilt sandwich and blind-stitch the binding in place over the machine-stitching line on the back side. Hand-mitre the corners on the back as shown in Figure 18.

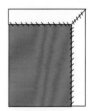

Figure 18

SUMMERSET KITCHEN COLLECTION

Sort your stash and find 15 coordinating fat quarters to create this colourful and easy-to-make table set.

Designs | Pearl Louise Krush

Project Specifications
Skill Level: Beginner
Placemat Size: 18" x 12"
Napkin Size: 14" x 14"
Coaster Size: 4½" x 4½"

Materials
1 fat quarter each white floral, blue floral, yellow tonal, blue tonal, red tonal, green tonal and light blue print
4 coordinating fat quarters for backings
4 coordinating fat quarters for napkins
1⅝ yards coordinating plaid
1 yard thin cotton batting
All-purpose thread to match coordinating plaid

Note
The fabrics listed will make four placemats, four napkins and four coasters.

Cutting
Cut four 4½" A squares for placemat centres and four 5" H squares for coasters from white floral.

Cut one 4½" x 21" strip yellow tonal; subcut strip into eight 2½" B strips.

Cut one 8½" x 21" strip light blue print; subcut strip into eight 2½" C strips.

Cut one 8½" x 21" strip red tonal; subcut strip into eight 2½" D strips.

Cut one 12½" x 21" strip blue tonal; subcut strip into eight 2½" E strips.

Cut one 12½" x 21" strip green tonal; subcut strip into eight 1½" F strips.

Cut one 12½" x 21" strip blue floral; subcut strip into eight 2½" G strips.

Cut four 21" x 15" placemat backings from coordinating fat quarters.

Cut one 14½" square each four coordinating fat quarters and four coordinating plaid for napkins.

Cut four 5" squares coordinating plaid for coaster backings.

Cut four 21" x 15" rectangles and four 5" squares batting.

Cut (10) 2¼" by fabric-width strips coordinating plaid for binding for all projects.

Placemats

Completing the Placemats
Fold each 21" x 15" backing piece vertically and horizontally, and crease to mark the centres.

Lay a 21" x 15" backing rectangle wrong side up on a flat surface; place a same-size batting piece on top.

Summerset Kitchen Collection

Fold A vertically and horizontally, and crease to mark the centre; centre A on the batting/backing layer, pinning through the centre of A to the creased centre of the backing; pin to hold in place.

Place a B strip right sides together on the top and bottom of A and stitch as shown in Figure 1; press B to the right side. *Note: Be careful when pressing; if batting is not heat-resistant, do not touch iron on batting.*

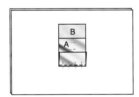

Figure 1

Repeat with C strips on opposite sides of A.

Repeat with D strips on the top and bottom.

Continue adding E, F and G strips to opposite sides to complete the pieced top.

Trim stitched top to 18½" x 12½".

Repeat instructions above to complete four placemats.

Join binding strips on short ends with angled seams to make one long strip as shown in Figure 2; trim seam to ¼". Press seams open.

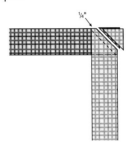

Figure 2

Fold strip with wrong sides together along length; press.

Sew binding to the right side of the runner edges, mitring corners and overlapping ends. Fold binding to the back side and stitch in place to finish.

Repeat binding steps to complete four placemats.

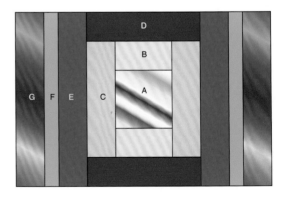

Summerset Placemat
Placement Diagram
18" x 12"

Coasters

Completing the Coasters

Sandwich a 5" batting square between a same-size backing square and an H square; pin to hold layers together.

Bind edges as for placemats to complete.

Repeat to complete four coasters. ∎

Summerset Coaster
Placement Diagram
4½" x 4½"

Napkins

Completing the Napkins

Lay a fat quarter napkin square right sides together with a coordinating plaid napkin square; stitch all around, leaving a 4" opening on one side.

Clip corners; turn right side out through opening.

Press opening edges ¼" to the inside; hand-stitch opening closed to complete one napkin.

Repeat to complete four napkins.

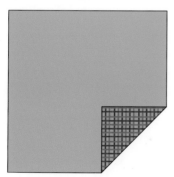

Summerset Napkin
Placement Diagram
14" x 14"

LAND & SEA BARGELLO PLACEMATS

Bring harmony to your daily dining. Set the tone with these tranquil placemats.

Design | Carolyn S. Vagts

Project Specifications
Skill Level: Beginner
Placemat Size: 18" x 13"

Materials
(8) 2½" x 42" coordinating/contrasting teal, green and blue strips
⅝ yard coordinating solid or mottled brown
2 backing rectangles 22" x 17"
2 batting rectangles 26" x 21"
Neutral-coloured all-purpose thread
Quilting thread

Note
The fabrics listed will make two placemats.

Cutting
Cut three 2½" by fabric-width strips coordinating solid or mottled brown; subcut strips into four 14½" A strips and four 13½" B strips.

Cut four 2¼" by fabric-width strips coordinating solid or mottled brown for binding.

Preparing the Bargello Panel
Lay out the 2½" x 42" strips on a table, making sure that there is a good contrast between them.

Assign each strip a number, starting at the top of the arrangement as shown in Figure 1.

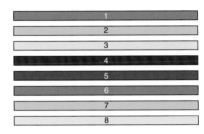

Figure 1

Starting with strips 1 and 2, join strips in numerical order in sets of two; press seams in the same direction from strip 1 to strip 8 or from strip 8 to strip 1.

Join the pairs to complete the strip set; press seams in the same direction.

Subcut the strip set into the following segments in the order given: 2½", 2", 1½", 2", 2½", 3", 2½" and 2½" as shown in Figure 2. Set aside remainder of strip set for second placemat.

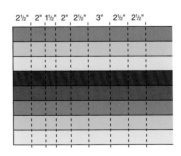

Figure 2

Land & Sea Bargello Placemats

Place segments 1 and 2 right side up and move segment 2 so that the pieces in the segments are offset by about half as shown in Figure 3. Place the segments right sides together as arranged and stitch to join as shown in Figure 4; press seam open.

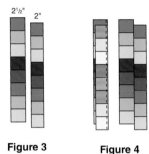

2½" 2"

Figure 3   **Figure 4**

Place segment 3 next to the pieced unit and move it up or down one piece as desired to create a pattern; sew to the previously stitched unit and press seam open.

Continue with remaining segments in the order cut until all segments are joined into one panel as shown in Figure 5. *Note: You should not move any segment up or down more than one or two pieces, or it will not create a pleasing pattern.*

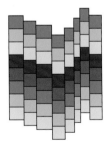

Figure 5

Trim the bargello panel to 14½" x 9½" as shown in Figure 6 to finish.

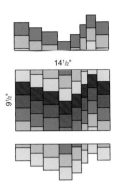

14½"

9½"

Figure 6

Repeat to complete two bargello panels.

Completing the Placemats

Sew A strips to opposite long sides and B strips to opposite short ends of each bargello panel; press seams toward A and B strips to complete the two placemats.

Layer, quilt and bind referring to Getting Ready to Quilt on pages 14–17. ■

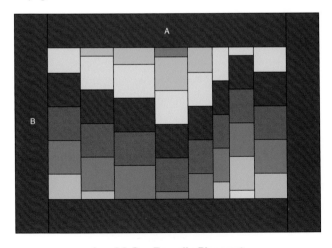

Land & Sea Bargello Placemat
Placement Diagram
18" x 13"

You can make a different version of the Land & Sea Bargello Placemats pattern using a bright and festive mix of spicy red and vibrant yellow, combined with a touch of green. A set of placemats in this colour combination will be the perfect table accessory at your next taco-night supper.

LOLLIPOP SPRING

This whimsical table runner has lots of colour and pizzazz. Depending on your choice of fabric for the appliqué pieces, the flowers will either pop off the table runner or nestle in a bed of spring florals.

Design | Wendy Sheppard

Project Specifications

Skill Level: Beginner
Runner Size: 38" x 18"
Block Size: 10" x 10"
Number of Blocks: 3

Materials

19 coordinating 2½" by fabric-width strips, including pink print, red print, blue print, white print, green print, brown tonal dot, white tonal dot and green tonal dot
10" squares: 3 red tonal dot, 1 white/red dot and 4 green tonal dot

Note: Some quilt shops offer precut 2½"-wide strip packages as well as precut 10" squares. With the use of these precuts, you can stitch this runner in an evening and use it on your table the next day.

Backing 42" x 22"
Batting 42" x 22"
Cream all-purpose thread
2 each ⅜" and ⅝" ladybug buttons
4 fusible web sheets 9" x 12"
1 yard ¼"-wide fusible web strips
⅜"-wide bias pressing bar
Quilting thread

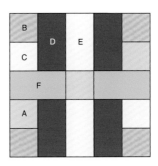

Lollipop Spring
10" x 10" Block
Make 3

Cutting

Cut nine 2½" A squares from one 2½"-wide blue print strip.

Cut (12) 2½" B squares from one 2½"-wide pink print strip.

Cut six 2½" C squares and six 4½" E rectangles from one 2½"-wide white print strip.

Cut (12) 4½" D rectangles from two 2½"-wide red print strips.

Cut six 4½" F rectangles from one 2½"-wide green print strip.

Select five white print and tonal dot 2½"-wide strips and trim to 1½" wide; subcut the trimmed strips into two 10½" G, two 32½" H and two 34½" J strips.

Lollipop Spring

Select one brown tonal dot 2½"-wide strip and trim to 1½" wide; subcut the trimmed strip into two 12½" I strips.

Select three brown tonal dot 2½"-wide strips; subcut strips into two 34½" K strips and two 18½" L strips.

Select three 2½"-wide green tonal dot strips for binding.

Trace flower and leaf shapes given on pages 30 and 31 onto the paper side of the fusible web, leaving ½" between pieces and referring to patterns for number to cut; cut out shapes, leaving a margin around each one.

Fuse shapes to the wrong side of the 10" squares as directed on pieces for colour; cut out shapes on traced lines. Remove paper backing.

Select one 2½"-wide strip green tonal dot for stems.

Completing the Lollipop Blocks

Sew A to B; press seam toward A. Repeat to make two A-B units.

Sew D to each A-B unit to make two A-B-D units as shown in Figure 1; press seams toward D.

Figure 1

Repeat to make two B-C-D units, again referring to Figure 1.

Join one each A-B-D and B-C-D units with E to make an E row as shown in Figure 2; press seams toward D. Repeat to make a second E row.

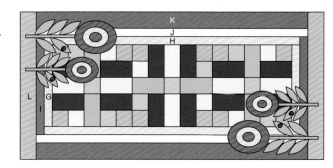

Lollipop Spring
Placement Diagram
38" x 18"

Figure 2

Sew A between two F pieces to make an A-F row as shown in Figure 3; press seams toward A.

Figure 3

Sew the A-F row between the two E rows to complete one Lollipop Spring block as shown in Figure 4; press seams toward the A-F row.

Figure 4

Repeat to complete a total of three Lollipop Spring blocks.

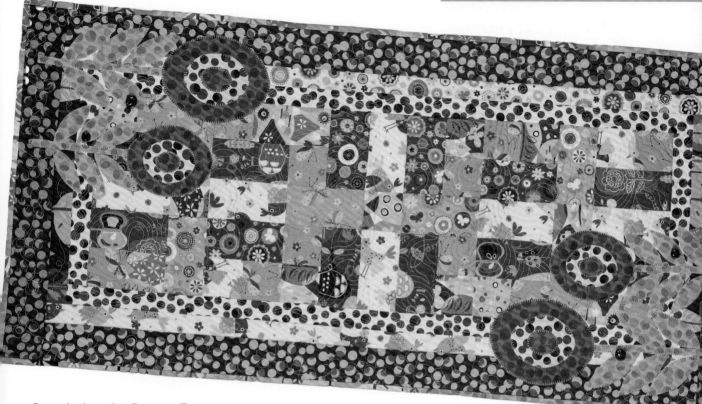

Completing the Runner Top

Arrange and join the three blocks as shown in Figure 5; press seams in one direction.

Figure 5

Sew G strips to opposite short ends and H strips to opposite long sides of the block centre; press seams toward G and H strips.

Sew I strips to opposite short ends and J strips to opposite long sides; press seams toward I and J strips.

Sew K strips to opposite long sides and L strips to opposite short ends to complete the pieced top; press seams toward K and L strips.

Completing the Appliqué

Trim the selected stem strip to 1½" wide; fold the strip with wrong sides together along length. Stitch raw edges together using a ¼" seam allowance.

After stitching, insert the bias pressing bar and centre and press seam open to complete the stem strip as shown in Figure 6.

Figure 6

Cut the stem strip into two 5¼" and two 6¾" lengths.

Apply ¼"-wide fusible web strip to the wrong side of each stem piece referring to the manufacturer's instructions.

Arrange and fuse one long stem, five large leaves and one large flower motif on the border area of one end of the pieced runner top, referring to the Placement Diagram for positioning of pieces.

Repeat with one short stem, six small leaves and one medium flower motif next to the large flower.

Repeat on the opposite end of the pieced runner top, again referring to the Placement Diagram for positioning.

Using cream thread and a medium-sized blanket stitch, sew all around each piece to secure.

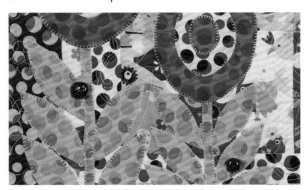

Completing the Runner

Layer, quilt and bind referring to Getting Ready to Quilt on pages 14–17.

Sew a ⅜" ladybug button to one small leaf on each small flower motif and a ⅝" ladybug button to one large leaf on each large flower motif to finish. ■

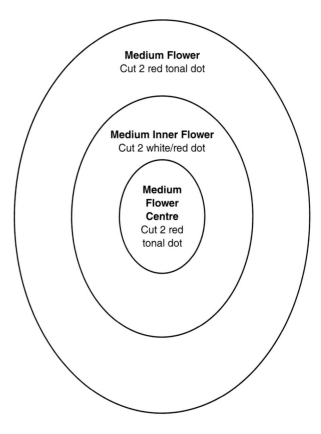

Medium Flower
Cut 2 red tonal dot

Medium Inner Flower
Cut 2 white/red dot

Medium
Flower
Centre
Cut 2 red
tonal dot

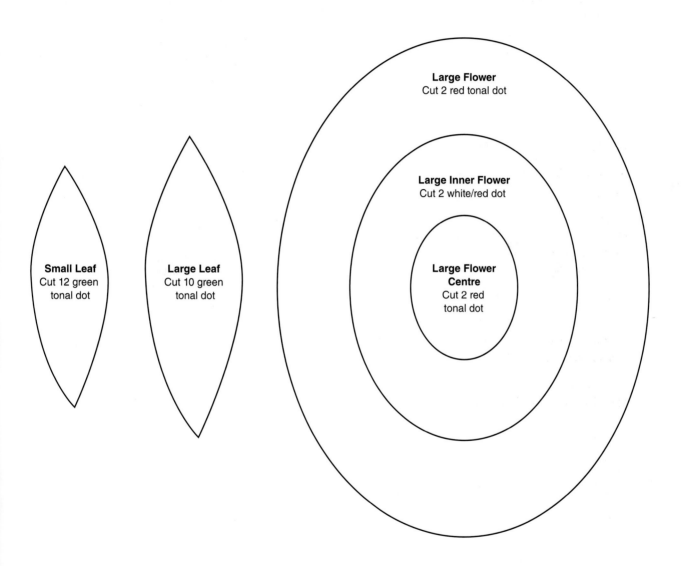

Small Leaf
Cut 12 green
tonal dot

Large Leaf
Cut 10 green
tonal dot

Large Flower
Cut 2 red tonal dot

Large Inner Flower
Cut 2 white/red dot

**Large Flower
Centre**
Cut 2 red
tonal dot

WATERMELON TABLE SET

A bright watermelon print is the perfect fabric for a summer table set.

Designs | Lucy Fazely

Project Specifications
Skill Level: Beginner
Runner Size: 50½" x 19½"
Placemat Size: 19½" x 11¾"
Napkin Size: 19" x 19"

Materials
¼ yard pink seed print
½ yard green stripe
⅝ yard black leaf print
⅝ yard black/white stripe
⅔ yard cream leaf print
⅔ yard red/white check
Runner backing 56" x 25"
2 placemat backings 25" x 18"
Runner batting 56" x 25"
2 placemat battings 25" x 18"
All-purpose thread to match fabrics
Clear nylon monofilament

Note
The fabrics listed will make one runner, two placemats and two napkins.

Cutting
Cut one 7½" by fabric-width strip pink seed print; subcut strip into four 7½" squares. Cut each square in half on one diagonal to make eight A triangles.

Cut one 13" by fabric-width strip green stripe; subcut strip into (16) 2½" B strips.

Cut two 10" by fabric-width strips cream leaf print; subcut strips into eight 10" squares. Cut each square in half on one diagonal to make 16 C triangles.

Cut seven 2½" by fabric-width strips black leaf print; set aside three strips for G borders. Subcut remaining strips into two 16" D pieces, four 8¼" E pieces and four 20" F pieces.

Cut one 20" by fabric-width strip red/white check; subcut strips into two 20" squares for napkins.

Cut eight 2¼" by fabric-width strips black/white stripe for binding.

Runner

Completing the Runner
Separate the B strips into sets of two, matching the stripe colour in each set as much as possible. Sew the lightest side of one B strip to one short side of A as shown in Figure 1; press seams toward B. Stitch a second B strip to the adjacent short side of the A-B unit, again referring to Figure 1; press seam toward B.

Figure 1

Watermelon Table Set

Trim excess B strips even with A as shown in Figure 2; repeat for eight A-B units.

Figure 2

Sew a C triangle to each B side of each A-B unit, extending C beyond the point of A-B as shown in Figure 3; press seams toward C.

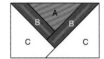

Figure 3

Trim each A-B-C unit to 16" x 8¼" as shown in Figure 4. Set aside two units for placemats.

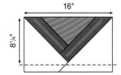

Figure 4

Join three A-B-C units as shown in Figure 5; press seams toward C edges; repeat for two pieced sections.

Figure 5

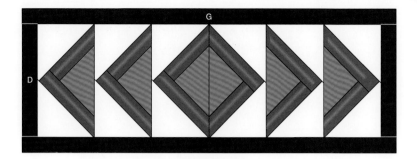

Watermelon Runner
Placement Diagram
50½" x 19½"

Watermelon Placemat
Placement Diagram
19½" x 11¾"

Join the two pieced sections to complete the pieced centre referring to the Placement Diagram for positioning; press seam open.

Sew D strips to opposite short ends of the pieced centre; press seams toward D.

Join the three G strips on short ends to make one long strip; subcut into two 51" G strips.

Sew G strips to opposite long sides of the pieced centre to complete the runner top; press seams toward G.

Sandwich runner batting between the completed top and prepared runner backing; pin or baste layers together to hold.

Machine-quilt as desired using clear nylon monofilament. When quilting is complete, trim batting and backing even with top; remove pins or basting.

Join binding strips on short ends to make one long strip. Fold the strip in half along length with wrong sides together; press.

Sew binding to runner edges with raw sides even, mitring corners and overlapping ends. Fold binding to the back side and stitch in place to finish. Set aside excess binding for placemats.

Placemats

Completing the Placemats

Sew E strips to opposite short ends of each remaining A-B-C unit; press seams toward E.

Sew F strips to opposite long sides of each pieced centre to complete the placemat tops; press seams toward F.

Sandwich placemat batting between the placemat top and backing, and complete placemats as for runner.

Napkins

Turn under the edges of each 20" napkin square ¼"; press. Turn under ¼" again; press and stitch to complete napkins. ■

WITH A TWIST OF ORANGE

Every meal will be a time to celebrate with these brightly coloured placemats. The matching wall quilt is an added bonus.

Designs | Julie Higgins

Wall Quilt

Project Specifications
Skill Level: Intermediate
Wall Quilt Size: 45" x 33"
Block Size: 6" x 6"
Number of Blocks: 24

Materials
24 coordinating 5" A squares
⅛ yard orange mottled
⅛ yard yellow mottled
⅛ yard lime green tonal
⅛ yard orange check
⅝ yard orange print
1 yard bright blue mottled
Batting 53" x 41"
Backing 53" x 41"
Neutral-coloured all-purpose thread
Quilting thread

Cutting
Prepare a template for B using pattern given on page 41; cut 96 from bright blue mottled. *Note: All pieces must be cut on the fabric the same way—there are no reverse or mirror-image shapes.* Place template right side up on the right side of the fabric when cutting all pieces.

Cut two 1½" x 36½" G strips and two 1½" x 26½" H strips bright blue mottled.

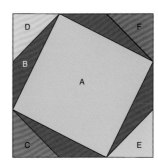

Twist
6" x 6" Block
Make 24 for quilt &
6 for each placemat

Cut one 2⅞" by fabric-width strip each orange mottled (C), yellow mottled (D), lime green tonal (E) and orange check (F); subcut each strip into (12) 2⅞" squares. Cut each square in half on one diagonal to make 24 each C, D, E and F triangles.

Cut two 4" x 38½" I strips and two 4" x 33½" J strips orange print.

Completing the Blocks
Sew a B piece to each side of an A square; press seams toward B. *Note: Match the ends of the seam allowances at the corners very carefully as shown in Figure 1.*

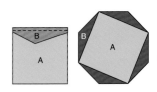

Figure 1

With a Twist of Orange

Sew one each C, D, E and F triangle to each A-B unit to complete 24 identical Twist blocks, placing the triangles in the same position on each block; press seams toward the triangles.

Completing the Top

Arrange and join six Twist blocks to make a row, orienting the triangles in the same position in the row as shown in Figure 2; press seams in one direction. Repeat to make four rows.

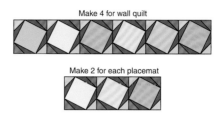

Make 4 for wall quilt

Make 2 for each placemat

Figure 2

Join the rows, alternating seam pressing from row to row, to complete the pieced centre; press seams in one direction.

Sew G strips to opposite long sides and H strips to opposite short ends of the pieced centre; press seams toward G and H strips.

Sew I strips to opposite long sides and J strips to opposite short ends of the pieced centre; press seams toward I and J strips.

Completing the Quilt

Fold the completed top horizontally and vertically, and crease to mark the side and end centres.

To mark scallop placement, measure and mark a point at the centre crease on the wrong side of the I strip 3¾" from seam as shown in Figure 3. Measure 1½" on one side of the crease and mark a point at the seam line; measure up 2⅜" from that point and mark to make the first dip in the scallop, again referring to Figure 3.

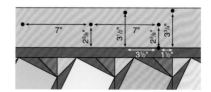

Figure 3

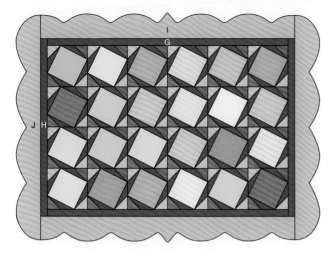

With a Twist of Orange Wall Quilt
Placement Diagram
45" x 33"

Measure and mark 7" from last marked inside point for the centre of the next dip in the scallop, again referring to Figure 3. Measure and mark a point 3½" from the 2⅜" point and 3½" from the seam to mark the centre of the scallop curve, referring to Figure 3. Repeat with a second 7" and 3½" measurement. Measure out 2⅜" and mark points for the scallop dips.

Repeat on the opposite side of the centre mark.

Draw centre peak from the 3¾" centre point to the 2⅜" points on either side, referring to Figure 4. Using a circular object, such as a plate, draw scallop shapes on the marked border strips as shown in Figure 4.

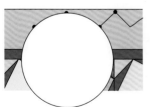 

Figure 4

Measure and mark a point at the centre crease of J strip 2⅜" and mark a point; measure and mark a point 7" on each side of the centre for the scallop dips as shown in Figure 5. Mark scallop shapes on each end of the pieced centre, and connect corners, again referring to Figure 5.

2⅜"

3½"

7"

Figure 5

Place the batting on a flat surface with the backing piece right side up on top; place the completed top right sides together with the backing. Stitch on the marked scallop line all around, leaving a 4" opening on one side. Trim excess to leave a ¼" seam allowance all around and clip into dips as shown in Figure 6.

Figure 6

Turn right side out through the opening; press edges flat. Turn opening edges in ¼" and hand-stitch closed; press.

Quilt as desired by hand or machine to finish.

Placemats

Project Specifications
Skill Level: Intermediate
Placemat Size: 27" x 21"
Block Size: 6" x 6"
Number of Blocks: 6 per placemat

Materials
12 coordinating 5" A squares
⅛ yard orange mottled
⅛ yard yellow mottled
⅛ yard lime green tonal
⅛ yard orange check
⅜ yard orange print
½ yard bright blue mottled
2 batting rectangles 31" x 25"
2 backing rectangles 31" x 25"
Neutral-coloured all-purpose thread
Quilting thread

Note
The fabrics listed will make two placemats.

Cutting
Prepare a template for B using pattern given; cut 48 from bright blue mottled. *Note: All pieces must be cut on the fabric the same way—there are no reverse or mirror-image shapes.* Place template right side up when cutting all pieces.

Cut two 1½" by fabric-width strips bright blue mottled; subcut strips into two 18½" K strips and two 14½" L strips.

Cut one 2⅞" by fabric-width strip each orange mottled (C), yellow mottled (D), lime green tonal (E) and orange check (F); subcut each strip into six 2⅞" squares. Cut each

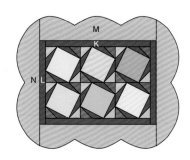

With a Twist of Orange Placemat
Placement Diagram
27" x 21"

square in half on one diagonal to make 12 each C, D, E and F triangles.

Cut two 4" by fabric-width strips orange print; subcut strips into two 20½" M strips and two 22½" N strips.

Completing the Blocks
Sew a B piece to each side of an A square; press seams toward B. *Note: Match the ends of the seam allowances at the corners very carefully as shown in Figure 1 (see page 36).*

Sew one each C, D, E and F triangle to each A-B unit to complete 12 identical Twist blocks, placing the triangles in the same position on each block; press seams toward the triangles.

Completing the Tops
To complete one placemat top, arrange and join three Twist blocks to make a row, orienting the triangles in the same position in the row, again referring to Figure 2 (see page 38); press seams in one direction. Repeat to make two rows.

Join the rows, with row seam pressing facing opposite directions, to complete the pieced centre; press seams in one direction.

Sew K strips to opposite long sides and L strips to opposite short ends of the pieced centre; press seams toward K and L strips.

Sew M strips to opposite long sides and N strips to opposite short ends of the pieced centre; press seams toward M and N strips.

Repeat to make second placemat.

Completing the Placemats

Refer to Completing the Quilt instructions on pages 38 and 39. Refer to Figure 7 to mark two scallops on each end, and one full and two partial scallops on each side of each placemat top, eliminating the centre peaks.

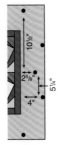

Figure 7

Place one batting rectangle on a flat surface with one backing piece right side up on top; place completed top right sides together with the backing. Stitch on the marked scallop line all around, leaving a 4" opening on one side. Trim excess to leave a ¼" seam allowance all around and clip into dips, again referring to Figure 6 (see page 39).

Turn right side out through the opening; press edges flat. Turn opening edges in ¼" and hand-stitch closed; press.

Quilt as desired by hand or machine to finish.

Repeat to complete the second placemat. ■

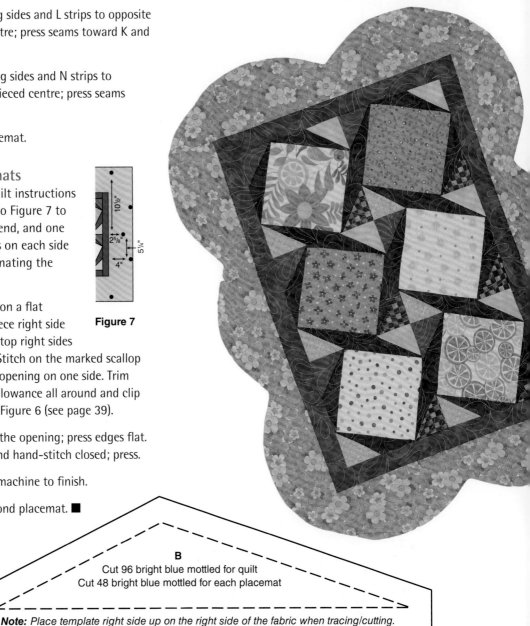

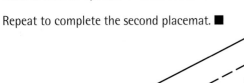

B
Cut 96 bright blue mottled for quilt
Cut 48 bright blue mottled for each placemat

Note: Place template right side up on the right side of the fabric when tracing/cutting.

STEPPING STONES

A simple piecing method makes this runner quick and easy to complete.

Design | Julie Weaver

Project Specifications
Skill Level: Beginner
Runner Size: 48" x 18"
Block Size: 10" x 10"
Number of Blocks: 4

Materials
½ yard cream tonal
⅔ yard cream floral
1¼ yards green tonal
Note: *Cream floral and green tonal must be 43" wide to complete border strips without piecing.*
Backing 54" x 24"
Batting 54" x 24"
Neutral-coloured all-purpose thread
Quilting thread

Cutting
Cut one 10½" by fabric-width strip cream tonal; subcut strip into four 10½" A squares.

Cut three 5½" by fabric-width strips green tonal; subcut strips into (16) 5½" B squares and four 3½" L squares.

Cut three 1½" by fabric-width strips green tonal; subcut strips into two 40½" D strips and two 12½" E strips.

Cut six 1" by fabric-width G/J strips green tonal.

Cut four 2¼" by fabric-width strips green tonal for binding.

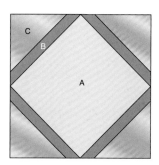

Stepping Stones
10" x 10" Block
Make 4

Cut six 1" by fabric-width F/I strips cream floral.

Cut three 1½" by fabric-width H/K strips cream floral.

Cut two 4½" by fabric-width strips cream floral; subcut strips into (16) 4½" C squares.

Completing the Blocks
Draw a diagonal line from corner to corner on the wrong side of each B and C square.

Place a C square right sides together on one corner of one B square; stitch on the marked line as shown in Figure 1.

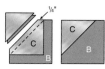

Figure 1

Stepping Stones

Trim seam to ¼" and press C to the right side to complete a B-C unit, again referring to Figure 1 (see page 42); repeat to make 16 B-C units.

To complete one Stepping Stones block, place a B-C unit right sides together on one corner of an A square as shown in Figure 2; stitch on the marked line. Trim seam to ¼" and press the B-C unit to the right side, again referring to Figure 2.

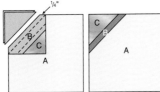

Figure 2

Repeat on each corner of A to complete one block; repeat to make four blocks.

Completing the Top

Join the four blocks to complete the pieced centre; press seams in one direction.

Sew D strips to opposite long sides and E strips to opposite short ends of the pieced centre; press seams toward D and E strips.

Join two each F/I and G/J strips with one H/K strip with right sides together along length to make a strip set as shown in Figure 3; press seams toward G/J. Repeat to make three strip sets. Trim two strip sets to 42½" for F-G-H. Cut two 12½" I-J-K strips from the remaining strip set.

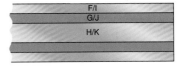

Figure 3

Sew F-G-H strips to opposite long sides of the pieced centre; press seams toward D strips.

Sew L squares to opposite end of I-J-K strips to make end strips as shown in Figure 4; press seams toward L.

Figure 4

Sew end strips to opposite short ends of the pieced centre to complete the pieced top.

Completing the Runner

Sandwich the batting between the completed top and prepared backing; pin or baste layers together.

Quilt as desired by hand or machine; remove pins or basting. Trim excess backing and batting even with runner top.

Join binding strips on short ends to make one long strip; press seams open. Fold the strip in half along length with wrong sides together; press.

Sew binding to the right side of the runner edges, mitring corners and overlapping ends. Fold binding to the back side and stitch in place to finish. ■

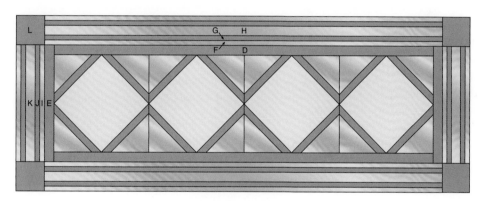

Stepping Stones
Placement Diagram
48" x 18"

COTTAGE CHARM COLLECTION

This sweet collection of quilted kitchen items is a great way to use the pretty floral prints from your fabric stash.

Designs | Pearl Louise Krush

Project Specifications

Skill Level: Beginner
Table Runner Size: 39½" x 17½"
Bun Warmer Size: 13½" x 18", before ties; fits 8" x 11" dish
Pot Holder Size: 9" x 9"
Tea Cozy Size: 11½" x 11½"

Materials

(37) 5" assorted print A squares
½ yard white tonal
1 yard coordinating stripe
1⅝ yards floral
Thin cotton batting 45" x 23" (table runner)
High-loft batting 14" x 18½" (bun warmer) and two 12" squares (tea cozy)
9½" square flame-retardant batting for pot holder
Matching and contrasting all-purpose thread
Quilting thread
½ yard ¼"-wide elastic
¼ yard fusible web
30" rayon cord
8" x 11" glass baking dish

Cutting

Cut eight 1½" by fabric-width strips white tonal; subcut strips into (14) 5" B strips, six 16" C strips, two 38" D strips and two 18" E strips.

Cut the following from the floral: three 2¼" by fabric-width strips for runner binding, one 45" x 23" rectangle for runner backing, one 9½" square for pot holder backing, and two 12" I squares for tea cozy.

Cut the following from the coordinating stripe: one 14" x 18½" F rectangle for bun warmer lining, two 1½" by fabric-width G/H strips for bun warmer ties and pot-holder hanger, two 12" J squares for tea cozy lining, and four 1½" x 12" K strips for tea cozy casings.

Trace appliqué shapes given on page 53 onto the paper side of the fusible web; cut out shapes, leaving a margin around each shape.

Fuse shapes to the wrong side of fabrics as directed on patterns for colour; cut out shapes on traced lines. Remove paper backing.

Cottage Charm Collection

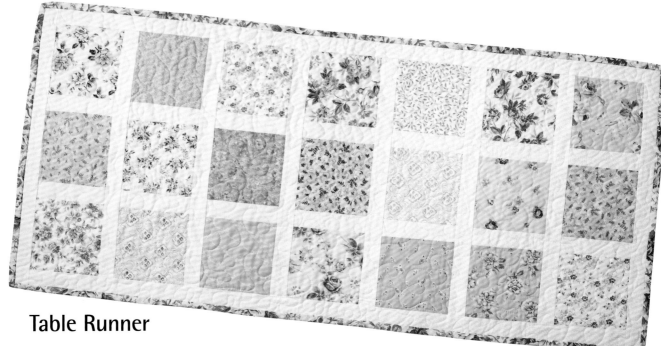

Table Runner

Completing the Table Runner

Arrange 21 A squares in seven rows of three in each row, mixing up the prints by scale and colour until the desired arrangement is achieved.

Keeping the squares as arranged, join three A squares with two B strips as shown in Figure 1; press seams toward A. Repeat with remaining A squares to complete seven A-B rows.

Join the A-B rows with C strips referring to the Placement Diagram for positioning to complete the pieced centre; press seams toward C strips.

Sew D strips to opposite long sides and E strips to opposite short ends of the pieced centre to complete the pieced top; press seams toward D and E strips.

Finishing the Table Runner

Sandwich batting between the completed top and prepared backing piece; pin or baste layers together to hold flat.

Quilt as desired by hand or machine; remove pins or basting. Trim batting and backing even with the top.

Figure 1

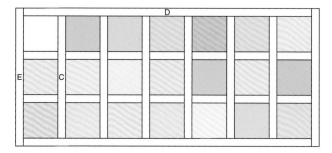

Cottage Charm Table Runner
Placement Diagram
39½" x 17½"

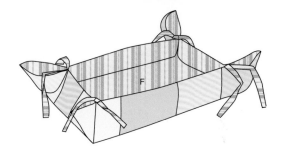

Cottage Charm Bun Warmer
Placement Diagram
13½" x 18", before ties

Join the binding strips with right sides together on short ends to make one long strip; press seams open.

Press the strip in half with wrong sides together along length.

Sew binding to the right side of the runner edges, mitring corners and overlapping ends.

Fold binding to the back side and stitch in place to finish.

Bun Warmer

Completing the Bun Warmer

Arrange 12 A squares in three rows of four squares each, mixing up the prints by scale and colour until the desired arrangement is achieved.

Join four A squares as arranged to make a row; press seams in one direction. Repeat to make three rows, pressing seams in the centre A row in the opposite direction from the other two rows.

Join the rows as arranged to complete the outside of the bun warmer (A unit).

Place the F lining rectangle right sides together with the A unit; place the layered unit with the A side on the 14" x 18½" rectangle high-loft batting; pin layers together at raw edges all around.

Sew all around outside edges, leaving a 4" opening on one side; clip corners. Trim batting close to seam.

Turn right side out through the opening; press.

Press opening edges to the inside ¼"; hand-stitch opening closed. Press again.

Machine-quilt in the ditch of seams.

Centre the rectangular baking dish on the lining side of the stitched unit.

Pinch each corner of the stitched unit to fit the corners of the dish as shown in Figure 2; pin together and hand-stitch to secure corners together.

Figure 2

Referring to Figure 3, fold the long raw edges of the G/H strips to the centre of the wrong side; press. Fold strips in half lengthwise and stitch along the double-folded edge.

Figure 3

Cut the stitched strips into four equal 12" G strips and one 6½" H strip. Fold the raw ends in ¼" and stitch across ends to complete G ties. Set aside H strip for pot holder.

Tie a knot in the centre of each G tie. Centre the knot at each pinched corner of the stitched unit and hand-stitch in place to secure and to hold corners together.

Tie each G tie into a bow at each corner to complete the bun warmer.

Cottage Charm Pot Holder
Placement Diagram
9" x 9"

Pot Holder

Completing the Pot Holder

Arrange four A squares in two rows of two squares each. Join A squares to make two rows; press seams in opposite directions. Join the rows to complete the pot-holder background; press seam in one direction.

Centre the appliqué teapot pieces diagonally on the pot-holder background, overlapping pieces as shown on pattern.

When satisfied with the arrangement, fuse shapes in place.

Using thread to match or contrast with pieces and a machine buttonhole stitch, sew around each shape.

Place the completed pot holder top right sides together with the 9½" backing square and place the layered unit on the 9½" batting square; pin raw edges together.

Stitch all around, leaving a 4" opening on one side; clip corners. Trim batting close to seam.

Turn right side out through the opening; press.

Press opening edges to the inside ¼"; hand-stitch opening closed. Press again. Quilt as desired.

Fold the H strip to make a loop; hand-stitch loop ends to the back side of one corner of the stitched pot holder to complete as shown in Figure 4.

Figure 4

Cottage Charm Tea Cozy
Placement Diagram
11½" x 11½"

Tea Cozy

Completing the Tea Cozy

Place an I square right sides together with a J lining square and place on one 12" square high-loft batting.

Stitch all around, leaving a 3" opening on one side; clip corners. Trim batting close to seam.

Turn right side out through the opening; press.

Press opening edges to the inside ¼"; hand-stitch opening closed. Press again.

Repeat with remaining I, J and 12"-square batting pieces to make a second I-J unit.

Fold the long edges and ends of the K casing strips under ¼"; press.

Pin the pressed K strips on the J side of the stitched I-J units 1½" from two opposite edges as shown in Figure 5; stitch along the long edges of each strip, again referring to Figure 5.

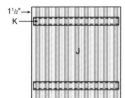

1½"→
K ——

J

Figure 5

Attach a safety pin to one end of the ¼"-wide elastic and thread through one casing of the I-J unit, out the other end and into the casing of the second I-J unit as shown in Figure 6; remove safety pin and stitch the ends of the elastic together to hold the I-J unit together at the bottom.

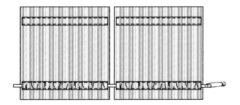

Figure 6

Thread cord though the remaining casings in the same manner as for elastic; knot each end of the cord to finish.

Place cozy over teapot with elastic at bottom. Pull cord to tighten around teapot to use. ■

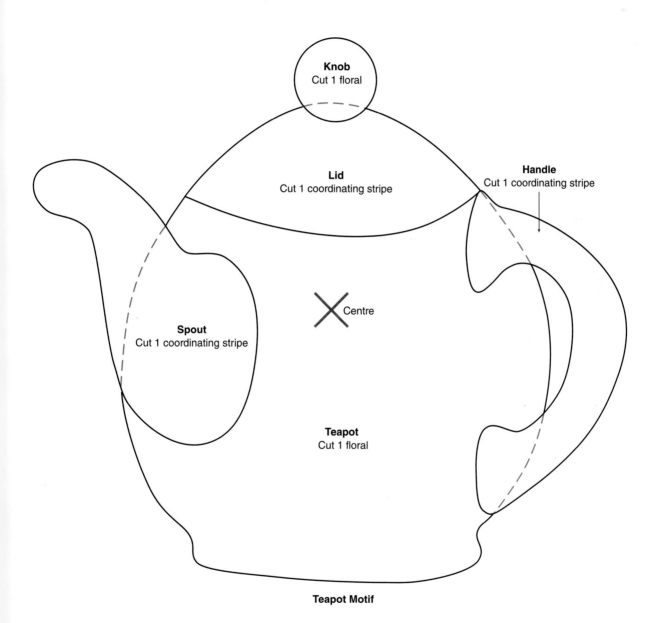

Knob
Cut 1 floral

Lid
Cut 1 coordinating stripe

Handle
Cut 1 coordinating stripe

Centre

Spout
Cut 1 coordinating stripe

Teapot
Cut 1 floral

Teapot Motif

SPRINGTIME TABLE MAT

The colours of springtime shine in this simple-to-stitch table mat.

Design | Connie Kauffman

Project Specifications
Skill Level: Beginner
Table Mat Size: 24" x 24"

Materials
¼ yard white tonal
⅓ yard dark blue tonal
⅓ yard yellow tonal
⅝ yard yellow/blue floral
Backing 27" x 27"
Batting 27" x 27"
All-purpose thread to match fabrics
Quilting thread

Cutting
Cut two 2" by fabric-width strips from white tonal; subcut strips into (32) 2" C squares.

Cut two 3½" by fabric-width strips from dark blue tonal; subcut strips into eight 5" F rectangles, four 6½" B rectangles and four 3½" E squares.

Cut one 2" by fabric-width strip and one 6½" A square from yellow tonal; subcut strip into (16) 2" H squares.

Cut one 6½" by fabric-width strip from yellow/blue floral; subcut strip into four 6½" D squares.

Cut one 3½" by fabric-width strip from yellow/blue floral; subcut strip into eight 2" G rectangles.

Cut one 9¾" square from yellow/blue floral. Cut square on both diagonals to make four I triangles.

Completing the Top
Mark a diagonal line from corner to corner on the wrong side of each C and H square.

Referring to Figure 1, place a C square right sides together on opposite ends of B; stitch on the marked lines.

Figure 1

Trim seams to ¼" and press C to the right side referring to Figure 2.

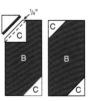

Figure 2

Springtime Table Mat

Repeat on the remaining corners of B referring to Figure 3, to complete one B-C unit; repeat to make four B-C units.

Make 4

Figure 3

Referring to Figure 4, sew C to one corner of F; trim seam to ¼" and press C to the right side. Repeat with a second C on the same end of F to complete one C-F unit, again referring to Figure 4. Repeat to complete eight C-F units.

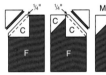

Make 8

Figure 4

Repeat with G and H to complete eight G-H units, referring to Figure 5.

Make 8

Figure 5

Sew a B-C unit to opposite sides of A as shown in Figure 6; press seams toward A.

Figure 6

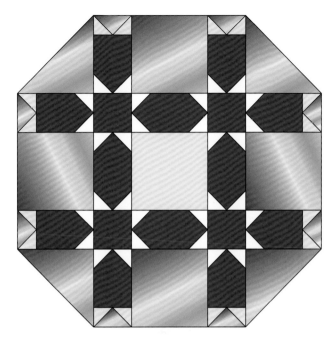

Springtime Table Mat
Placement Diagram
24" x 24"

Sew an E square to opposite ends of each of the remaining two B-C units as shown in Figure 7; press seams toward E.

Figure 7

Sew a B-C-E unit to the remaining sides of A to complete the centre unit as shown in Figure 8; press seams away from A.

Figure 8

Sew a G-H unit to the F end of a C-F unit as shown in Figure 9; press seam toward C-F. Repeat to make eight C-F-G-H units.

Make 8

Figure 9

Sew a C-F-G-H unit to opposite sides of D to make a side unit as shown in Figure 10; press seams toward D. Repeat to make four side units.

Make 4

Figure 10

Sew a side unit to opposite sides of the centre unit to complete the centre row as shown in Figure 11; press seams toward the side units.

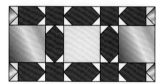

Figure 11

Sew I to each end of each remaining side unit to make the top row as shown in Figure 12; press seams toward I. Repeat to make the bottom row.

Figure 12

Sew the top and bottom rows to the centre row to complete the pieced top; press seams away from the centre row.

Completing the Table Mat

Lay the batting square on a flat surface with the backing square right side up on top; place the pieced top right sides together with the backing square and pin layers to hold.

Trim excess batting and backing edges even with the pieced top; stitch all around, leaving a 5" opening on one side.

Turn right side out through the opening and press flat.

Press opening seams to the inside ¼"; hand-stitch opening closed.

Hand- or machine-quilt as desired to finish. ∎

COUNTRY GARDEN

Create a flower garden for your table with pretty floral prints.

Design | Connie Kauffman

Project Specifications
Skill Level: Beginner
Runner Size: 33" x 21"
Block Size: 6" x 6"
Number of Blocks: 4

Materials
¼ yard dark burgundy floral
¼ yard tan floral
¼ yard burgundy/peach print
¼ yard peach tonal
¼ yard green tonal
Backing 39" x 27"
Batting 39" x 27"
Neutral-coloured all-purpose thread
Quilting thread

Cutting
Cut one 6½" A square dark burgundy floral with large motif centred.

Cut four 3½" C squares from smaller floral sections of the dark burgundy floral.

Cut six 6½" F squares tan floral with large motif centred in each square.

Cut two 3½" by fabric-width strips burgundy/peach print; subcut strips into (30) 2" E rectangles.

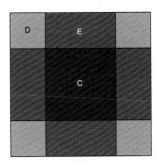

Uneven Nine-Patch
6" x 6" Block
Make 4

Cut two 2" by fabric-width strips peach tonal; subcut strips into (40) 2" D squares.

Cut one 3⅜" by fabric-width strip green tonal; subcut strip into three 3⅜" squares. Cut each square on both diagonals to make 12 G triangles.

Cut two 2" by fabric-width strips green tonal; subcut strips into (28) 2" B squares.

Completing the Blocks
To complete one Uneven Nine-Patch block, sew E to opposite sides of C as shown in Figure 1 to make a C-E unit; press seams toward C.

Figure 1

Country Garden

Sew D to opposite ends of E as shown in Figure 2; press seams toward E. Repeat to make two D-E units.

Make 2

Figure 2

Sew D-E units to opposite long sides of the C-E unit to complete one block; press seams toward the D-E units.

Repeat to complete four Uneven Nine-Patch blocks.

Completing the Top

Mark a diagonal line from corner to corner on the wrong side of each B square.

Place a B square right sides together on each corner of A and stitch on the marked lines as shown in Figure 3; trim seams to ¼" and press B to the right side to complete one A-B unit, again referring to Figure 3.

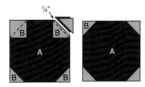

Figure 3

Repeat with B and F to complete six B-F units as shown in Figure 4.

Make 6

Figure 4

Sew D to each end of E; press seams toward E. Repeat to make 10 D-E units.

Sew a D-E unit to one side of a B-F unit to make an end unit as shown in Figure 5; press seams toward the B-F unit. Repeat to make six end units.

Make 6

Figure 5

Join two end units with one Uneven Nine-Patch block to make the top row as shown in Figure 6; press seams away from the end units. Repeat to make the bottom row.

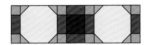

Figure 6

Join the A-B unit with two Uneven Nine-Patch blocks and two end units to make the centre row as shown in Figure 7; press seams toward the Uneven Nine-Patch blocks.

Figure 7

Sew G to each end of a D-E unit as shown in Figure 8; press seams toward G. Repeat to make four D-E-G units.

Make 4

Figure 8

Sew D to one end of E and add G to make a G-D-E unit as shown in Figure 9; press seams toward E and G; repeat to make two units and two reverse units, again referring to Figure 9.

Figure 9

Sew two D-E-G units and one each G-D-E unit and reverse G-D-E unit to the top and bottom rows referring to Figure 10; press seams away from the rows.

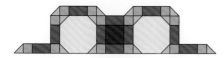

Figure 10

Sew the top and bottom rows to the centre row to complete the pieced top; press seams away from the centre row.

Completing the Runner

Place backing piece right side up on batting; place completed top right sides together with backing; pin edges.

Trim backing and batting even with the pieced top.

Sew all around, leaving a 4" opening along one side; clip corners. Trim batting close to stitching.

Turn right side out through opening; press edges flat.

Turn opening edges in ¼"; hand-stitch opening closed.

Quilt as desired by hand or machine to finish. ∎

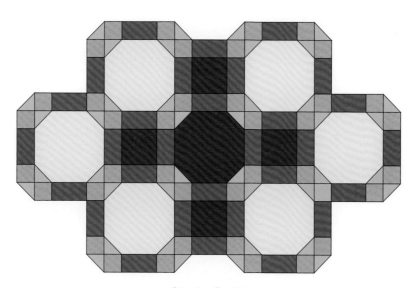

Country Garden
Placement Diagram
33" x 21"

CHARMED RUNNER & COASTERS

Have fun stitching this very scrappy runner and matching coasters from colourful print fabrics.

Designs | Chris Malone

Runner

Project Specifications
Skill Level: Beginner
Runner Size: 51" x 12¾"

Materials
(22) 5" A squares coordinating print
2 each 5" squares rose and yellow print
(4) 5" squares green print
⅓ yard brown solid
½ yard brown print
Backing 59" x 20"
Batting 59" x 20"
All-purpose thread to match fabrics
Quilting thread
Pink and yellow size 8 pearl cotton
½ yard lightweight nonwoven interfacing
¼"-wide bias pressing bar

Note
Some quilt shops carry precut 5" squares in coordinating colours. This is a perfect project for their use.

Cutting
Cut 1⅛"-wide bias strips from brown solid to total 45" when seamed for vines.

Cut 2¼"-wide bias strips from brown print to total 170" when seamed for binding.

Completing the Runner
Arrange and join the A squares into six inside rows with three A squares each, and two end rows with two A squares each, referring to Figure 1. Press seams in adjacent rows in opposite directions.

Figure 1

Join the stitched rows in staggered rows as arranged to complete the pieced background; press seams in one direction.

Completing the Appliqué
Prepare templates using patterns given on page 67.

Draw a total of 16 leaf shapes onto the wrong side of the 5" green print squares, leaving a margin of at least ¼" between the shapes.

Pin each traced square traced-side up onto the lightweight nonwoven interfacing; stitch all around each traced leaf on drawn lines. Cut out each shape ⅛" from the stitching line; clip curves and tips as shown in Figure 2.

Figure 2

Charmed Runner & Coasters

Cut a slash through the interfacing side only referring to pattern for positioning; turn each leaf right side out through the slashed opening. Press edges flat.

Using the same method as for leaves, prepare five rose and four yellow flower shapes using the 5" rose and yellow print squares. Repeat with flower centres using leftover pieces from flowers, cutting five yellow and four rose centres.

Fold the brown solid bias vine strip in half with wrong sides together along length; stitch a scant ¼" seam down the length. Trim seam to ⅛"; insert the bias pressing bar and press seam open with seam running down the centre of the length as shown in Figure 3.

Figure 3

Referring to the Placement Diagram and project photo, arrange the vine in gentle curves down the length of the table runner, beginning and ending the vine about 4" from the corners of the ends of the runner; baste or pin and hand-stitch in place.

Pin a centre to each flower; hand-stitch in place. *Note: When appliquéing using this interfacing method, stitch through the edge of the fabric, not the interfacing.*

Arrange and hand-stitch the nine flowers along the vine with a rose flower at the centre and at each end of the vine and the remaining flowers alternating and evenly spaced in between. Arrange and hand-stitch the leaves in place referring to the Placement Diagram for positioning.

Charmed Runner
Placement Diagram
51" x 12¾"

Using 1 strand of pearl cotton, make three French knots in the centre of each flower, using pink for the rose flowers and yellow for the yellow flowers.

Completing the Runner

Sandwich the batting between the completed top and the prepared backing; pin or baste together to hold.

Quilt as desired by hand or machine; remove pins or basting. Trim excess backing and batting even with the edge of the runner top. *Note: The sample was machine-quilted, stitching in the ditch around each appliqué shape. In addition, the leaf pattern was used to stitch a stem and leaf shape in the open squares as shown in Figure 4.*

Figure 4

Join the brown print bias binding strips on the short ends with diagonal seams to make one long strip as shown in Figure 5. Trim seams to ¼" and press open. Fold the strip in half with wrong sides together along length; press carefully to avoid stretching.

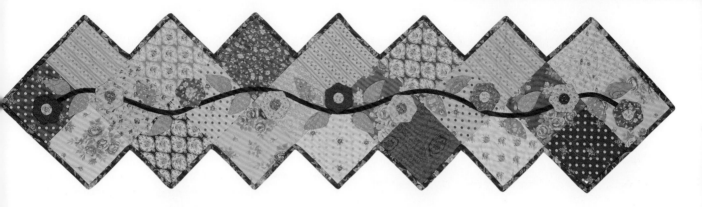

Figure 5

Bind edges referring to Finishing the Edges on pages 16 and 17. *Note: When approaching an inside corner, pin the binding mitre to the right side, and then mirror the mitre on the back side and stitch in place, adding a few stitches to the mitre fold on the front and back as shown in Figure 6.*

Figure 6

Coasters

Project Specifications
Skill Level: Beginner
Coaster Size: 4½" x 4½"

Materials
(8) 5" squares coordinating print
1 each 5" square rose, yellow and green prints
1 fat quarter brown solid
⅓ yard brown print
(4) 6" squares batting
All-purpose thread to match fabrics
Quilting thread
Pink and yellow size 8 pearl cotton
¼ yard lightweight nonwoven interfacing
¼"-wide bias pressing bar

Note
The fabrics listed will make four coasters.

Cutting

Cut four 1⅛" x 6" bias strips brown solid for vines.

Cut three 2¼" by fabric-width strips brown print for binding.

Completing the Appliqué

Prepare templates using patterns given.

Draw four leaf shapes onto the wrong side of the 5" green print square, leaving a margin of at least ¼" between the shapes. *Note: For variety, more than one square of green print may be used.*

Pin each traced square traced-side up onto the lightweight nonwoven interfacing; stitch all around each traced leaf on drawn lines. Cut out each shape ⅛" from the stitching line; clip curves and tips as shown in Figure 2 (see page 62).

Cut a slash through the interfacing side only, referring to pattern for positioning; turn each leaf right side out through the slashed opening. Press edges flat.

Prepare the two each rose and yellow flower shapes in the same manner as leaves using the 5" rose and yellow print squares. Repeat with flower centres using leftover pieces from flowers.

Fold each brown solid bias vine strip in half with wrong sides together along length; stitch a scant ¼" seam down the length. Trim seam to ⅛"; insert the bias pressing bar and press seam open with seam running down the centre of the length as shown in Figure 3 (see page 64).

Select one of the coordinating print 5" squares for coaster front; mark a point 3" up from the bottom right corner and another point 4" to the left of the corner as shown in Figure 7.

Figure 7

Pin the ends of one vine piece at these points and curve the centre section into a gentle arc as shown in Figure 8; pin to hold. Hand-stitch the vine piece in place.

Figure 8

Arrange and hand-stitch a leaf and then a flower shape along the vine, referring to the Placement Diagram for positioning of pieces. *Note: When appliquéing using this interfacing method, stitch through the edge of the fabric, not the interfacing.*

Using 1 strand of pearl cotton, make three French knots in the centre of each flower, using pink for the rose flowers and yellow for the yellow flowers.

Completing the Coasters
Sandwich a 6" batting square between the completed top and a 5" coordinated print backing square; pin or baste together to hold.

Quilt as desired by hand or machine; remove pins or basting. Trim excess backing and batting even with the edges of the coaster top. *Note: The sample was machine-quilted, stitching in the ditch around each appliqué shape.*

Join the binding strips on the short ends with diagonal seams to make one long strip as shown in Figure 5 (see page 65). Trim seams to ¼" and press open. Fold the strip in half with wrong sides together along length; press.

Bind edges referring to Finishing the Edges on pages 16 and 17. ■

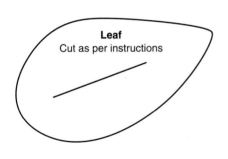

Leaf
Cut as per instructions

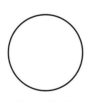

Flower Centre
Cut as per instructions

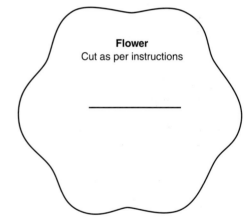

Flower
Cut as per instructions

SUMMER PICNIC PLACEMATS

*Add some sizzle to your summer picnic
with these colourful placemats.*

Design | Connie Kauffman

Project Specifications
Skill Level: Beginner
Placemat Size: 16" x 12"

Materials
Scraps navy blue prints, tonals or mottleds
Scraps red prints, tonals or mottleds
1 fat quarter white speckled print
2 backing rectangles 20" x 16"
2 batting rectangles 20" x 16"
Neutral-coloured all-purpose thread

Cutting
Cut (16) 2½" A squares, (12) 2⅞" D squares and four 2⅞"
E squares from variety of navy blue print, tonal or mottled
scraps. Cut E squares in half on one diagonal to make
eight E triangles.

Cut (16) 2⅞" C squares and four 2⅞" F squares from
variety of red print, tonal or mottled scraps. Cut the F
squares in half on one diagonal to make eight F triangles.

Cut four 2⅞" x 21" strips from white speckled print;
subcut strips into (28) 2⅞" B squares.

Completing the Pieced Units
Draw a diagonal line from corner to corner on the wrong
side of each B square.

Place a B square right sides together with a C square;
stitch ¼" on each side of the marked line as shown in
Figure 1.

Figure 1

Cut apart on the marked line to make two B-C units as
shown in Figure 2; press seams toward C.

Make 16

Figure 2

Repeat to complete 32 B-C units.

Repeat with B and D to complete 24 B-D units.

Summer Picnic Placemats

Completing the Placemats

Arrange and join A squares, E and F triangles, and the B-C and B-D units in rows as shown in Figure 3; press seams toward darker fabric pieces. *Note: Arrange so that same-fabric pieces do not touch.*

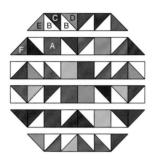

Figure 3

Summer Picnic Placemats
Placement Diagram
16" x 12"

Join the rows, again referring to Figure 3; press seams away from the centre row to complete the top.

Repeat to complete the second placemat top.

Layer batting, backing right side up and pieced top right side down and pin. Trim batting and backing even with the pieced top.

Stitch all around, leaving a 3" opening on one side; trim batting close to seam. Turn right side out through opening.

Press seam opening ¼" to the inside; hand-stitch opening closed.

Quilt as desired by hand or machine to finish. ∎

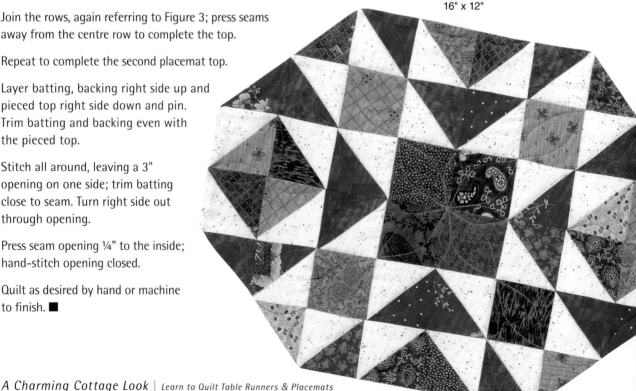

CHRISTMAS LOG RUNNER

Just two sizes of Log Cabin blocks combine to make this large traditional table runner.

Design | Sandra L. Hatch

Specifications

Skill Level: Beginner
Runner Size: 59" x 20¾"
Block Sizes: 12" x 12" and 7½" x 7½"
Number of Blocks: 3 and 4

Materials

¼ yard red holly check
¼ yard cream star tonal
⅓ yard dark red print
⅓ yard green print
⅓ yard green star tonal
⅝ yard green holly check
⅔ yard red print
Backing 67" x 29"
Batting 67" x 29"
All-purpose thread to match fabrics
Quilting thread
Rotary rulers with 45- and 90-degree-angle marks

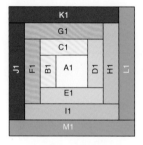

Large Log Cabin
12" x 12" Block
Make 3

Small Log Cabin
7½" x 7½" Block
Make 4

Cutting

Cut one 2" by fabric-width strip red print; subcut strip into three each 3½" B1 and 5" C1 pieces.

Cut one 1½" by fabric-width strip red print; subcut strip into four each 2" B2 and 3" C2 pieces.

Cut three 2⅜" by fabric-width strips red print; subcut strips into eight 11¾" N pieces. Using the rotary ruler with 45-degree-angle mark, trim ends of each N piece at a 45-degree angle as shown in Figure 1.

Figure 1

Cut two 3⅜" by fabric-width strips red print; subcut strips into two each 12½" P and 15⅜" Q strips.

Cut two 2" by fabric-width strips red holly check; subcut strips into three each 6½" F1 and 8" G1 pieces.

Cut one 1½" by fabric-width strip red holly check; subcut strip into four each 4" F2 and 5" G2 pieces.

Cut two 2" by fabric-width strips dark red print; subcut strips into three each 9½" J1 and 11" K1 pieces.

Cut two 1½" by fabric-width strips dark red print; subcut strips into four each 6" J2 and 7" K2 pieces.

Cut one 2" by fabric-width strip green holly check; subcut strip into three each 5" D1 and 6½" E1 pieces.

Cut one 1½" by fabric-width strip green holly check; subcut strip into four each 3" D2 and 4" E2 pieces.

Cut five 2¼" by fabric-width strips green holly check for binding.

Cut two 2" by fabric-width strips green star tonal; subcut strips into three each 8" H1 and 9½" I1 strips.

Cut two 1½" by fabric-width strips green star tonal; subcut strips into four each 5" H2 and 6" I2 pieces.

Cut two 2" by fabric-width strips green print; subcut strips into three each 11" L1 and 12½" M1 strips.

Cut two 1½" by fabric-width strips green print; subcut strips into four each 7" L2 and 8" M2 pieces.

Cut one 5½" by fabric-width strip cream star tonal; subcut strip into four 5½" squares. Cut each square in half on one diagonal to make eight O triangles. Cut the remainder of the strip into three 3½" x 3½" A1 squares and four 2" x 2" A2 squares.

Completing the Blocks

To complete one Large Log Cabin block, sew B1 to A1; press seam toward B1.

Add C1 to the A-B unit as shown in Figure 2; press seam toward C1.

Figure 2

Continue adding lettered D1 through M1 pieces around A1 in alphabetical order, pressing seams toward the newly added piece after stitching to complete one Large Log Cabin block referring to the block drawing. Repeat to make three Large Log Cabin blocks.

Christmas Log Runner

Repeat previous steps to complete four Small Log Cabin blocks using A2 through M2 pieces.

Completing the Runner

Sew O to N as shown in Figure 3; press seam toward N. Repeat to make eight N-O units.

Figure 3

Sew P to the M side of one Large Log Cabin block and to the K side of a second large block as shown in Figure 4; press seams toward P.

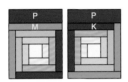

Figure 4

Sew Q to the L side of the P-M block and to the J side of the P-K block as shown in Figure 5; press seams toward Q.

Figure 5

Sew an N-O unit to the J and M sides of a Small Log Cabin block to make a side unit as shown in Figure 6; press seams toward the N-O units. Repeat to make four side units.

Figure 6

Arrange the side units with the remaining unbordered large block and the two bordered large blocks in diagonal rows referring to Figure 7; join to make rows. Press seams in adjacent rows in opposite directions.

Figure 7

Join the rows, stopping stitching at the end of the N-O seam as shown in Figure 8; press seams in one direction. *Note: The angled ends of the centre N pieces will be unstitched at this point.*

Figure 8

Fold the pieced top in half with the unstitched angled ends right sides together as shown in Figure 9. Place ruler matching ¼" line with N-O seam intersection, referring to Figure 10.

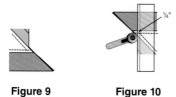

Figure 9   **Figure 10**

Starting at inside edge of N, cut to make a 90-degree angle, again referring to Figure 10. Repeat on the opposite side of the runner.

Stitch ¼" from cut edge and press seam open as shown in Figure 11. Repeat on both sides to complete a straight side on each side centre as shown in Figure 12.

Figure 11   **Figure 12**

Layer, quilt and bind referring to Getting Ready to Quilt on pages 14–17. ■

Christmas Log Runner
Placement Diagram
59" x 20¾"

HOORAY FOR HOLIDAYS

Dress your holiday table with this fun set of placemats and napkins. Use a coordinated set of fat quarters and make them reversible.

Designs | Reeze L. Hanson

Project Specifications
Skill Level: Beginner
Placemat Size: 17½" x 13½"
Napkin Size: 13½" x 13½"

Materials
20 coordinating fat quarters
Thin batting 22" x 18" for each placemat
Neutral-coloured all-purpose thread
Quilting thread
Basting spray or safety pins
Water-erasable marker

Note
The fabrics listed will make at least four placemats and four napkins. The instructions are written for making one of each.

Cutting
Select eight coordinating fat quarters for one placemat and napkin set. Designate which fat quarter will be used for the A centre, B ends, C pocket, D pocket edge, E binding and F backing; the remaining two fat quarters will be used for the napkin. *Note: You may mix and match fabrics to use the same fabric as the D fabric for binding, or the backing may be cut from the remaining D fabric. Save all remaining fabric pieces to combine and use for more placemats.*

Cut one 14" A square from the A fabric.

Cut two 2½" x 14" B rectangles from the B fabric.

Cut one 10" square from the C fabric; cut in half on one diagonal to make two C triangles.

Cut one 1½" x 15" D strip from the D fabric.

Cut and piece 2¼" bias strips from the E fabric to make an 80"-long strip.

Cut one 14" square from each of the remaining fat quarters for the napkin.

Placemat

Completing the Placemat
Sew B strips to opposite ends of A; press seams toward B strips.

Mark diagonal crosshatch lines 1¾" apart on the A-B top using a water-erasable marker as shown in Figure 1.

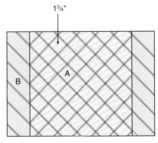

Figure 1

Sandwich the batting between the A-B top and the F backing fat quarter with right sides out; apply basting spray or use safety pins to hold layers together.

Stitch on the marked lines; remove marker lines. *Note: A walking foot may be used on your machine to keep layers from shifting.*

Trim the backing and batting edges even with the A-B top.

Fold and press the 1½"-wide D strip in half with wrong sides together along length.

Pin the pressed D strip along the diagonal of a C triangle, matching raw edges as shown in Figure 2.

Figure 2

Place the second C triangle right sides together on top of the pinned C-D unit; stitch together along the long diagonal edge as shown in Figure 3.

Figure 3

Hooray for Holidays
Placement Diagram
17½" x 13½"

Press one C to the wrong side and D up and away from the C pieces. Trim excess D to match C as shown in Figure 4.

Figure 4

Align the edges of the C-D pocket with one corner of the quilted A-B top and machine-baste in place as shown in Figure 5.

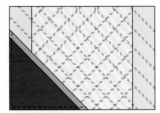

Figure 5

Bind the placemat referring to Finishing the Edges on pages 16 and 17.

Napkin

Completing the Napkin

Place the two 14" napkin squares right sides together, aligning edges.

Stitch all around, leaving a 3" opening on one side.

Clip corners; turn right side out through the opening.

Press opening edges ¼" to the inside.

Topstitch layers together close to the edge, closing the opening at the same time.

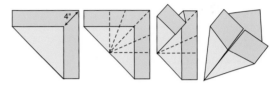

Figure 6

Fold napkin as shown in Figure 6 and place inside the placemat pocket. ■

WINTER FUN

*Make a seasonal pieced runner
with a matching wall quilt to
brighten those short winter days.*

Designs | Jill Reber

Table Runner

Project Specifications
Skill Level: Beginner
Runner Size: 36" x 21"

Materials
1 fat quarter each tan 1, tan 2, blue, burgundy skate,
    cream and red star prints
⅜ yard cream snowflake print
⅓ yard blue/cream check
¼ yard blue snowflake print
⅜ yard burgundy solid
Backing 42" x 27"
Batting 42" x 27"
All-purpose thread to match fabrics
Quilting thread
1½ yards 18"-wide fusible web
1 yard fabric stabilizer

Cutting
Cut one 5½" x 21" strip from tan 1 print; subcut strip into
three 5½" B1 squares.

Cut one 5½" x 21" strip from tan 2 print; subcut strip into
three 5½" B2 squares.

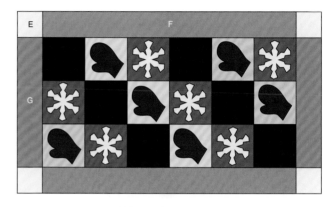

Winter Fun Runner
Placement Diagram
36" x 21"

Cut two 3½" x 15½" G strips from blue print.

Cut two 5½" x 21" strips from burgundy skate print;
subcut strips into six 5½" C squares.

Cut one 3½" by fabric-width strip from cream snowflake
print; subcut strip into four 3½" E squares.

Cut two 3½" x 30½" F strips from blue/cream check.

Cut one 5½" by fabric-width strip from blue snowflake
print; subcut strip into six 5½" A squares.

Cut four 2¼" by fabric-width strips from burgundy solid
for binding.

Winter Fun

Completing the Appliqué

Trace mitten and snowflake shapes given on page 85 onto the paper side of the fusible web referring to patterns for number to cut; cut out shapes leaving a margin around each one.

Fuse shapes to the wrong side of fabrics as directed on patterns for colour; cut out shapes on traced lines. Remove paper backing.

Centre and fuse each snowflake shape to an A square.

Centre and fuse a mitten shape to each B1 and B2 square.

Cut (12) 5½" squares fabric stabilizer; pin a square on the wrong side of each A, B1 and B2 square.

Using thread to match appliqué fabrics, machine zigzag-stitch around each mitten and snowflake shape; remove fabric stabilizer.

Completing the Runner

Join two each C squares, one each B1 and B2 mitten squares and two snowflake squares to make one each X, Y and Z row referring to Figure 2; press seams toward C squares.

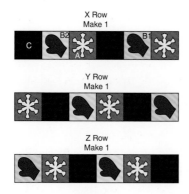

X Row
Make 1

Y Row
Make 1

Z Row
Make 1

Figure 2

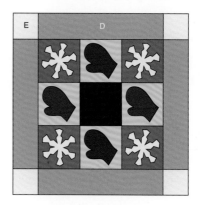

Winter Fun Wall Quilt
Placement Diagram
21" x 21"

Join the rows referring to the Placement Diagram to complete the pieced centre; press seams in one direction.

Sew F strips to opposite long sides; press seams toward F strips.

Sew E to each end of each G strip; press seams toward G strips.

Sew an E-G strip to opposite short ends of the pieced centre to complete the pieced top; press seams toward E-G strips.

Layer, quilt and bind referring to Getting Ready to Quilt on pages 14–17.

Wall Quilt

Project Specifications
Skill Level: Beginner
Quilt Size: 21" x 21"

Materials
Scrap red print
1 fat quarter each tan, cream, burgundy skate and
   red star prints

¼ yard blue snowflake print
¼ yard burgundy solid
⅓ yard blue/cream check
⅜ yard cream snowflake print
Backing 27" x 27"
Batting 27" x 27"
All-purpose thread to match fabrics
Quilting thread
1½ yards 18"-wide fusible web
1 yard fabric stabilizer

Cutting
Cut two 5½" x 21" strips from tan print; subcut strips into four 5½" B squares.

Cut one 5½" C square from burgundy skate print.

Cut one 3½" by fabric-width strip from cream snowflake print; subcut strip into four 3½" E squares.

Cut two 3½" by fabric-width strips from blue/cream check; subcut strips into four 15½" D strips.

Cut one 5½" by fabric-width strip from blue snowflake print; subcut strip into four 5½" A squares.

Cut two 2¼" by fabric-width strips from burgundy solid for binding.

Completing the Appliqué

Trace mitten and snowflake shapes given onto the paper side of the fusible web referring to patterns for number to cut; cut out shapes leaving a margin around each one.

Fuse shapes to the wrong side of fabrics as directed on patterns for colour; cut out shapes on traced lines. Remove paper backing.

Centre and fuse each snowflake shape to an A square.

Centre and fuse a mitten shape to each B square.

Cut eight 5½" squares fabric stabilizer; pin a square on the wrong side of each A and B square.

Using thread to match appliqué fabrics, machine zigzag-stitch around each mitten and snowflake shape; remove fabric stabilizer.

Completing the Wall Quilt

Join one mitten square with two snowflake squares to make a snowflake row as shown in Figure 1; press seams toward the mitten square. Repeat to make two snowflake rows.

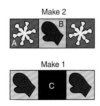

Make 2

Make 1

Figure 1

Join C square with two mitten squares to make a mitten row, again referring to Figure 1; press seams toward C.

Join the snowflake and mitten rows referring to the Placement Diagram to complete the pieced centre; press seams in one direction.

Sew D strips to opposite sides of the pieced centre; press seams toward D.

Sew an E square to each end of each remaining D strip; press seams toward D strips.

Sew D-E strips to the remaining sides of the pieced centre to complete the pieced top; press seams toward D-E strips.

Layer, quilt and bind referring to Getting Ready to Quilt on pages 14–17. ■

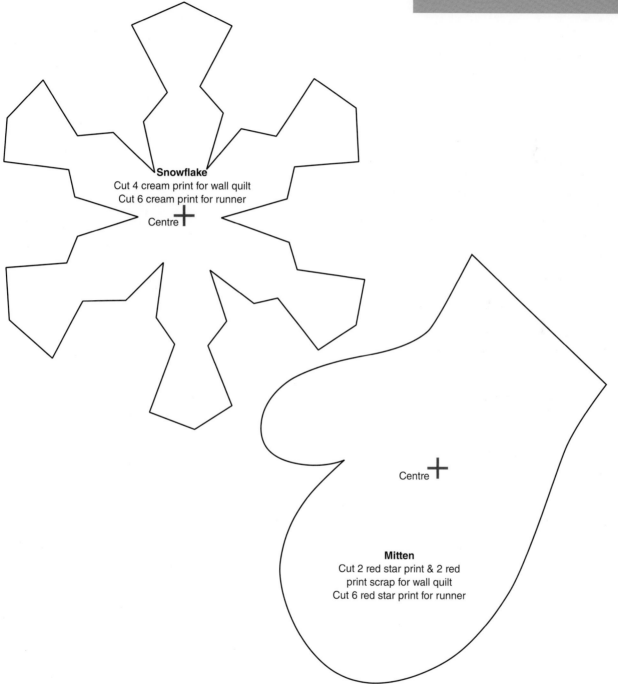

Snowflake
Cut 4 cream print for wall quilt
Cut 6 cream print for runner

Centre

Mitten
Cut 2 red star print & 2 red
print scrap for wall quilt
Cut 6 red star print for runner

Centre

HEARTS AFLOAT

Shades of pink create the pieced hearts floating in this soft runner.

Design | Sandra L. Hatch

Project Specifications

Skill Level: Beginner
Runner Size: Approximately 48½" x 18½"
Block Size: 10" x 10"
Number of Blocks: 3

Materials

4 fat quarters pink print
2 fat quarters (or ½ yard) white-with-pink print
Backing 52" x 22"
Batting 52" x 22"
White all-purpose thread
Pink quilting thread
Clear nylon monofilament

Cutting

Cut one 3" x 22" strip each from three different pink prints and three 3" x 22" strips from white-with-pink print.

Cut two 5½" A squares each from three different pink prints and three 5½" A squares from white-with-pink print.

Cut one 1¾" x 22" strip white-with-pink print; subcut strip into (12) 1¾" B squares.

Cut one 15⅜" square white-with-pink print; cut the square on both diagonals to make four C triangles.

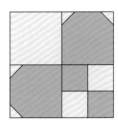

Hearts Afloat
10" x 10" Block
Make 3

Cut one each 2½" x 10½" D strip from two different pink prints.

Cut two 2½" x 12½" E strips from remaining pink print.

Cut two each 2½" x 22" F strips from two pink prints.

Completing the Blocks

Sew a pink print strip to a white-with-pink print strip with right sides together along length; press seams toward darker fabric. Repeat for three strip sets.

Subcut each strip set into 3" segments as shown in Figure 1; you will need two segments of each combination.

Figure 1   **Figure 2**

Hearts Afloat

Join two same-fabric segments to make a Four-Patch unit as shown in Figure 2; repeat for three units. Press seams in one direction.

Draw a diagonal line from corner to corner on the wrong side of each B square.

Place one B square right sides together with one pink print A square as shown in Figure 3; stitch on drawn line. Repeat on an adjacent corner, again referring to Figure 3.

Figure 3

Trim seams to ¼" beyond stitching line and press B to the right side to complete an A-B unit referring to Figure 4; repeat for six A-B units.

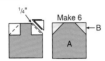

Figure 4

Join two same-fabric A-B units with one white-with-pink print A and one same-fabric Four-Patch unit to complete one Hearts Afloat block as shown in Figure 5; repeat for three blocks. Press seams in one direction.

Figure 5

Completing the Top
Sew C triangles to the pieced blocks as shown in Figure 6; press seams toward C. Join these pieced sections to complete the pieced centre; press seams toward C.

Figure 6

Sew a D strip to one side of end block as shown in Figure 7. Sew an E strip to the remaining side, again referring to Figure 7; press seam toward strip. Repeat on opposite end block.

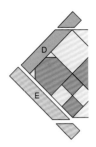

Figure 7

Cut excess strips at an angle even with side edges, again referring to Figure 7.

Join two different-fabric F strips on short ends to make a long strip; repeat. Referring to Figure 8, centre seam of strips with centre blocks and pin in place with right sides together. Stitch along length; press seams toward strips. Referring again to Figure 8, trim excess ends of each strip even with angle of previous strip to complete the pieced top.

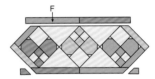

Figure 8

Completing the Runner
Layer, quilt and bind referring to Getting Ready to Quilt on pages 14–17. *Note: The sample was hand-quilted in the C triangles using the heart quilting design given and machine-quilted in the ditch of some block seams and ¼" inside seams using pink quilting thread. Clear nylon*

monofilament was used in the top of the machine and all-purpose thread in the bobbin to quilt in the ditch of border seams and between blocks.

Cut five 2¼" x 22" strips from remaining pink print fat quarter; join strips on short ends to make binding strip. Bind referring to Finishing the Edges on pages 16 and 17. ■

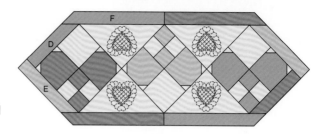

Hearts Afloat
Placement Diagram
48½" x 18½"

Heart Quilting Design

BLUE SKY AUTUMN

Pieced leaf shapes float on a blue background in this pretty autumn runner.

Design | Bea Yurkerwich

Project Specifications
Skill Level: Beginner
Runner Size: 52" x 20"
Block Size: 8" x 8"
Number of Blocks: 5

Materials
5 fat eighths in bright autumn colours
½ yard blue mottled
⅝ yard gold print
⅝ yard leaf-print batik
Backing 58" x 26"
Batting 58" x 26"
Neutral-coloured all-purpose thread
Quilting thread
¾ yard brown ¼"-wide fusible bias tape

Cutting
Prepare template for A/AR using pattern given on page 93; cut as directed.

Cut one 4½" by fabric-width strip blue mottled; subcut strip into five 4½" C squares.

Cut three 2⅞" by fabric-width strips blue mottled; subcut strips into (30) 2⅞" squares. Cut each square in half on one diagonal to make 60 B triangles.

Cut two 2½" x 40½" D strips gold print.

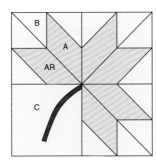

Leaf
8" x 8" Block
Make 5

Cut two 2½" x 12½" E strips gold print.

Cut four 2¼" by fabric-width strips gold print for binding.

Cut three 4½" by fabric-width strips leaf-print batik. Join strips with right sides together on short ends to make one long strip; press seams open. Subcut strips into two 44½" F strips.

Cut one 4½" by fabric-width strip leaf-print batik; subcut strip into two 20½" G strips.

Completing the Leaf Blocks
To complete one Leaf block, select three each same-fabric A and AR pieces. Referring to Figure 1 (see page 92), sew B to one angled end of A; add a second B to complete an A-B unit. Press seams. Repeat to make three A-B units.

Blue Sky Autumn

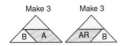

Make 3   Make 3

Figure 1

Repeat to complete three AR-B units, again referring to Figure 1.

Join one each A-B and AR-B unit to make a block quarter as shown in Figure 2; press seams to one side. Repeat to make three block quarters.

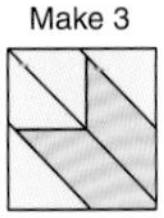

Make 3

Figure 2

Cut the fusible bias tape into five 4½" lengths; arrange and fuse one length to each C square referring to the block drawing for placement.

Join two block quarters to make a row as shown in Figure 3; press seam in opposite direction than the C row.

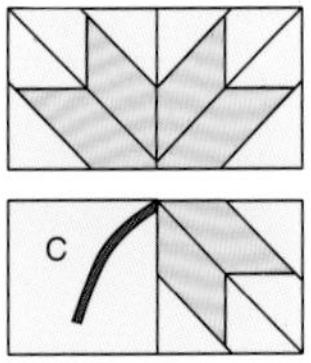

Figure 3

Sew a C square to one block quarter to make a row, again referring to Figure 3; press seam toward C.

Join the rows to complete one Leaf block; press seam in one direction.

Repeat to complete five Leaf blocks (one from each fat eighth).

Completing the Top

Arrange and join the Leaf blocks referring to the Placement Diagram for positioning to complete the pieced centre; press seams in one direction.

Sew D strips to opposite long sides and E strips to opposite short ends of the pieced centre; press seams toward D and E strips.

Sew F strips to opposite long sides and G strips to opposite short ends of the pieced centre to complete the pieced top; press seams toward F and G strips.

Completing the Runner

Mark the vein quilting pattern onto each A/AR piece.

Sandwich the batting between the completed top and prepared backing; pin or baste layers together to hold.

Quilt on vein lines and as desired by hand or machine; remove pins or basting. Trim excess backing and batting even with runner top.

Join binding strips on short ends to make one long strip; press seams open. Fold the strip in half along length with wrong sides together; press.

Sew binding to the right side of the runner edges, mitring corners and overlapping ends. Fold binding to the back side and stitch in place to finish. ■

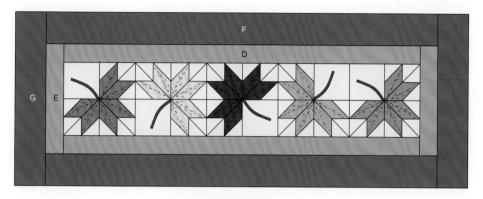

Blue Sky Autumn
Placement Diagram
52" x 20"

Vein Quilting Pattern

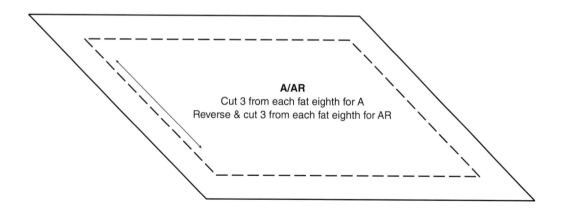

A/AR
Cut 3 from each fat eighth for A
Reverse & cut 3 from each fat eighth for AR

AUTUMN LEAVES & PUMPKINS

Small appliquéd pumpkins and leaves create the design of this autumn runner.

Design | Barbara Clayton

Project Specifications
Skill Level: Beginner
Runner Size: 38¾" x 15½"
Block Size: 5½" x 5½"
Number of Blocks: 13

Materials
Scraps bright orange, dark orange, rust, green and gold prints
¼ yard cream tonal
¼ yard tan/cream print
¼ yard light tan print
¼ yard dark tan print
⅓ yard dark brown/black print
⅓ yard chocolate brown print
Backing 45" x 22"
Batting 45" x 22"
All-purpose thread to match fabrics
Clear .004 nylon thread
Quilting thread
½ yard 12"-wide fusible web
½ yard fabric stabilizer
Water-erasable marker or pencil

Pumpkin
5½" x 5½" Block
Make 3

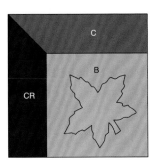

Leaf
5½" x 5½" Block
Make 10

Cutting
Cut three 6" A squares cream tonal.

Cut 4½" B squares as follows: two tan/cream print, four light tan print and four dark tan print.

Prepare template for C/CR using pattern given on page 98; cut as directed, marking the dot from pattern onto each piece using a water-erasable marker or pencil.

Completing the Leaf Blocks
Sew a C and CR to two adjacent sides of each B square, stopping stitching at marked dot. Align angled sides of C and CR, and stitch from dot to pointed ends. Press straight seams toward B and angled seams toward CR.

Autumn Leaves & Pumpkins

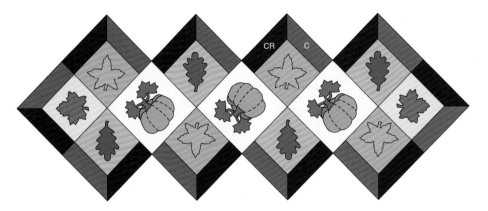

Autumn Leaves & Pumpkins
Placement Diagram
38¾" x 15½"

Trace oak, maple and sweet gum leaf shapes given on page 99 onto the paper side of the fusible web, referring to patterns for number to cut; cut out shapes, leaving a margin around each one. Fuse shapes to the wrong side of scraps as directed; cut out shapes on traced lines. Remove paper backing.

Arrange and fuse one leaf shape to each B-C-CR square referring to the Placement Diagram for positioning.

Cut (10) 4" squares fabric stabilizer; pin a square to the wrong side of each fused square.

Using a close satin stitch and thread to match leaf shapes, machine-stitch around each leaf shape to complete the 10 Leaf blocks.

Completing the Pumpkin Blocks
Prepare pumpkin appliqué shapes given on page 98 as for Leaf block shapes.

Referring to the patterns and block drawing, arrange and fuse shapes to the A squares in numerical order.

Cut three 5" squares fabric stabilizer; pin a square to the wrong side of each fused A square.

Machine-stitch pumpkin appliqué pieces in place as in Completing the Leaf Blocks to complete three Pumpkin blocks.

Completing the Top
Arrange and join the completed blocks in rows as shown in Figure 1; press seams in adjacent rows in opposite directions.

Figure 1

Join the rows as stitched to complete the pieced top; press seams in one direction.

Completing the Runner

Place backing piece right side up on batting; place completed top right sides together with backing; pin edges.

Trim backing and batting even with the pieced top.

Sew all around, leaving a 4" opening along one side; clip inner corners. Trim batting close to stitching.

Turn right side out through opening; press edges flat.

Turn opening edges to the inside ¼"; hand-stitch opening closed.

Quilt as desired by hand or machine to finish. ■

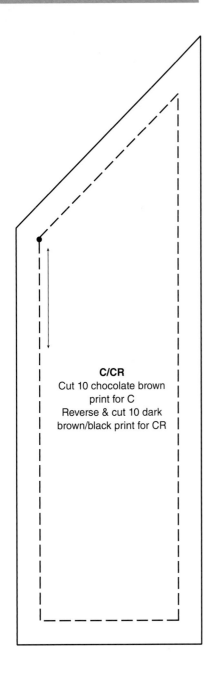

C/CR
Cut 10 chocolate brown
print for C
Reverse & cut 10 dark
brown/black print for CR

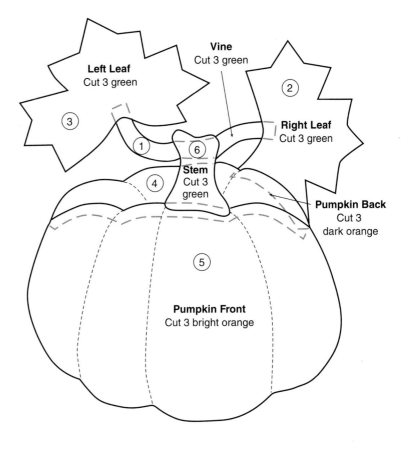

Left Leaf
Cut 3 green

Vine
Cut 3 green

③

①

Right Leaf
Cut 3 green

②

⑥

④

Stem
Cut 3
green

Pumpkin Back
Cut 3
dark orange

⑤

Pumpkin Front
Cut 3 bright orange

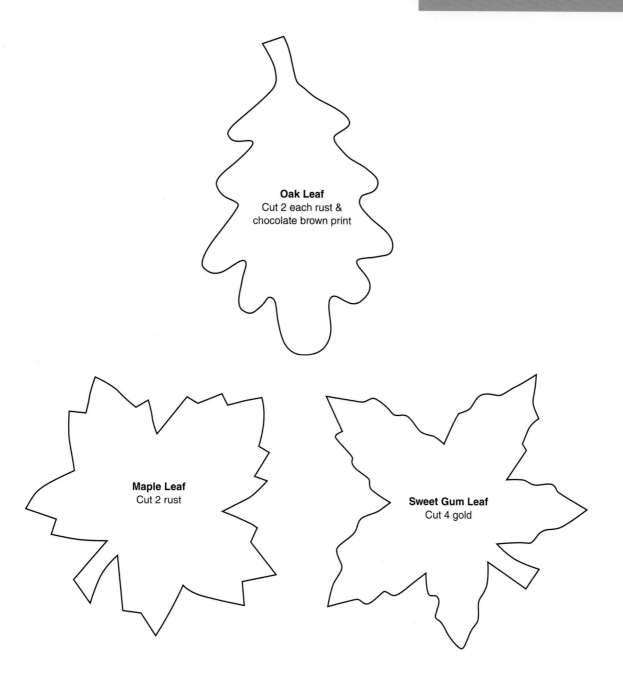

Oak Leaf
Cut 2 each rust &
chocolate brown print

Maple Leaf
Cut 2 rust

Sweet Gum Leaf
Cut 4 gold

FOUR-PANEL TABLE RUNNER

Cover every side of the table with this four-part table runner.

Design | Phyllis Dobbs

Project Specifications

Skill Level: Beginner
Runner Size: 62" x 62"
Block Size: 10" x 10"
Number of Blocks: 5

Materials

¼ yard gold print
⅓ yard coordinating stripe
½ yard gold tonal
½ yard gold floral
1 yard green print
(1) 16" x 68" and (2) 16" x 29" backing rectangles
(1) 16" x 68" and (2) 16" x 29" batting rectangles
Neutral-coloured all-purpose thread
Quilting thread
Clear ruler with 45-degree-angle line

Cutting

Cut one 10½" by fabric-width strip gold floral; subcut strip into four 10½" D squares.

Cut two 5⅞" by fabric-width strips gold tonal; subcut strips into (20) 2¾" B rectangles. Cut each B rectangle from the right end diagonally from the bottom corner to the top edge at a 45-degree angle as shown in Figure 1.

Figure 1

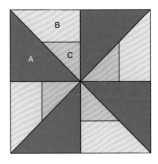

Pinwheel
10" x 10" Block
Make 5

Cut one 3⅝" by fabric-width strip gold print; subcut strip into (10) 3⅝" squares. Cut each square in half on one diagonal to make 20 C triangles.

Cut two 5⅞" by fabric-width strips green print; subcut strips into (10) 5⅞" squares. Cut each square in half on one diagonal to make 20 A triangles.

Cut seven 2¼" by fabric-width strips green print for binding.

Cut three 2½" by fabric-width strips coordinating stripe; subcut strip into (12) 10½" E strips.

Four-Panel Table Runner

Completing the Blocks

Sew B to C to make a B-C unit as shown in Figure 2; press seam toward C. Repeat to make 20 B-C units.

Make 20

Figure 2

Sew a B-C unit to A to complete an A-B-C unit as shown in Figure 3; press seam toward A. Repeat to make 20 A-B-C units.

Make 20

Figure 3

To complete one Pinwheel block, join two A-B-C units to make a row as shown in Figure 4; repeat to make two rows. Press seams in opposite directions.

Make 2

Figure 4

Join the rows referring to the block drawing to complete one block; press seam in one direction.

Repeat to complete five Pinwheel blocks.

Completing the Top

Join one Pinwheel block with one D square and three E strips to make a side unit as shown in Figure 5; press seams toward E. Repeat to make four side units.

Make 4

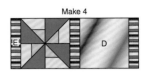

Figure 5

Sew a side unit to each side of the remaining Pinwheel block to complete the runner top.

Completing the Runner

Centre and sew a 16" x 29" backing piece to opposite sides of the 16" x 68" backing piece to make a backing piece to match the pieced top as shown in Figure 6; repeat with batting pieces.

Figure 6

Sandwich the batting between the completed top and prepared backing; pin or baste layers together.

Quilt as desired by hand or machine; remove pins or basting. Trim excess backing and batting even with runner top.

Join binding strips on short ends to make one long strip; press seams open. Fold the strip in half along length with wrong sides together; press.

Sew binding to the right side of the runner edges, mitring corners and overlapping ends. Fold binding to the back side and stitch in place to finish. ∎

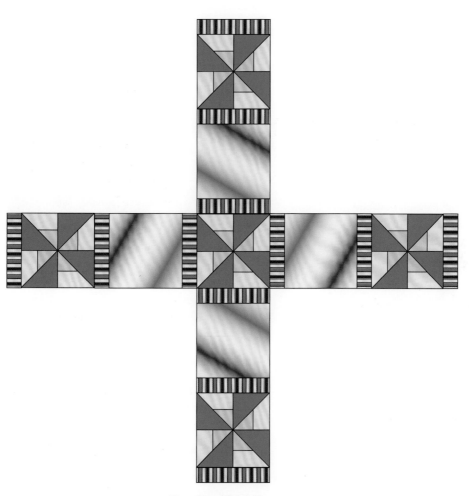

Four-Panel Table Runner
Placement Diagram
62" x 62"

CHINA BLUE TOPPER

The striking hexagonal shape and blue floral fabrics add a lovely traditional touch to your table.

Design | Julie Weaver

Project Specifications

Skill Level: Beginner
Topper Size: 36" x 36"
Block Size: 9" x 9"
Number of Blocks: 4

Materials

1 fat quarter each light and medium blue prints
1 fat quarter white/blue dot
½ yard white/blue floral
⅔ yard small dark blue floral
⅔ yard large dark blue floral
Batting 44" x 44"
Backing 44" x 44"
All-purpose thread to match fabrics
Quilting thread

Cutting

Cut one 4¼" x 21" strip white/blue dot; subcut strip into four 4¼" B squares.

Cut one 2⅜" x 21" strip white/blue dot; subcut strip into eight 2⅜" G squares.

Cut four 2" x 21" strips white/blue dot; subcut strips into (32) 2" F squares.

Cut one 3⅞" by fabric-width strip large dark blue floral; subcut strip into eight 3⅞" D squares.

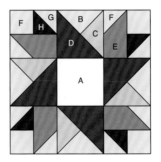

China Blue 1
9" x 9" Block
Make 2

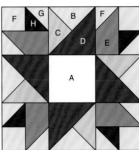

China Blue 2
9" x 9" Block
Make 2

Cut four 4" by fabric-width strips large dark blue floral; subcut each strip into one 15" L strip and one 25" M strip.

Cut one 2⅜" by fabric-width strip small dark blue floral; subcut strip into eight 2⅜" H squares.

Cut four 1½" by fabric-width strips small dark blue floral; subcut strips into eight 21" K strips.

Cut four 2¼" by fabric-width strips small dark blue floral for binding.

Cut two 3½" x 21" strips medium blue print; subcut strips into (16) 2" E rectangles.

Cut one 4¼" x 21" strip light blue print; subcut strip into four 4¼" C squares.

China Blue Topper

Cut one 14" by fabric-width strip white/blue floral; subcut strip into one 14" square, one 9½" J square and four 3½" A squares. Cut the 14" square on both diagonals to make four I triangles.

Completing the Blocks

Draw a diagonal line on the wrong side of each B and G square and 16 F squares.

Place a marked B square right sides together with a C square and sew ¼" on each side of the marked line as shown in Figure 1.

Figure 1

Cut apart on the drawn line and press C to the right side to complete two B-C units as shown in Figure 2.

Figure 2

Repeat to complete eight B-C units.

Draw a diagonal line across the seam on the wrong side of each B-C unit as shown in Figure 3.

Figure 3

Place each of these squares right sides together with a D square and sew ¼" on each side of the marked line as shown in Figure 4.

Figure 4

Cut apart on the marked lines, and press D to the right side to make eight B-C-D units and eight reversed B-C-D units as shown in Figure 5.

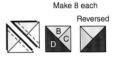

Figure 5

Repeat with marked G squares and H squares, referring to Figures 1 and 2, to complete 16 G-H units as shown in Figure 6.

Figure 6

Place a marked F square right sides together on one end of E and stitch on the marked line as shown in Figure 7.

Figure 7

Trim seam to ¼" and press F to the right side to complete an E-F unit, again referring to Figure 7.

Repeat to make 16 E-F units.

To complete one China Blue 1 block, select one A square and four each B-C-D units, F squares, G-H units and E-F units.

Sew F to the H side of a G-H unit as shown in Figure 8; press seam toward F. Add an E-F unit to complete one corner unit as shown in Figure 9; press seam toward the E-F unit. Repeat to make four corner units.

Make 4

Figure 8 **Figure 9**

Sew a B-C-D unit between two corner units to make a row as shown in Figure 10; repeat to make two rows. Press seams toward the B-C-D units.

Make 2

Figure 10

Sew an A square between two B-C-D units to make the centre row as shown in Figure 11; press seams toward A.

Figure 11

Referring to the block drawing, sew the centre row between the two previously pieced rows to complete the China Blue 1 block; press seams toward the centre row.

Repeat to complete a second China Blue 1 block.

Repeat with the reversed B-C-D units referring to Figure 12 to complete two China Blue 2 blocks.

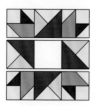

Figure 12

Completing the Top

Sew a J square between the two China Blue 2 blocks to make the centre row as shown in Figure 13; press seams toward J.

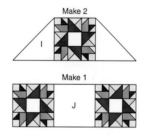

Make 2

Make 1

Figure 13

Sew an I triangle to opposite sides of each China Blue 1 block to make two I rows as shown in Figure 13; press seams toward I.

Sew an I row to opposite sides of the centre row to complete the pieced centre; press seams toward the centre row.

Centre and sew a K strip to each I side of the pieced centre as shown in Figure 14; press seams toward K strips.

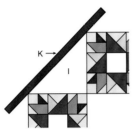

Figure 14

Trim excess K strips at each end even with the blocks using a straightedge as shown in Figure 15.

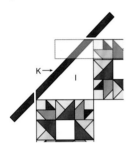

Figure 15

Repeat with remaining K strips on the block sides of the pieced centre, trimming ends at an angle with outer edges of K strips on I sides, referring to Placement Diagram.

Repeat with L strips first and then M strips to complete the pieced top; press seams toward L and M strips.

Layer, quilt and bind referring to Getting Ready to Quilt on pages 14–17. ■

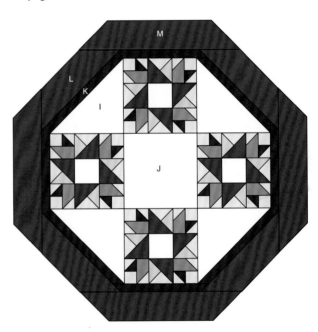

China Blue Topper
Placement Diagram
36" x 36"

BLOOMING ROSES

Piece together this elegant ensemble to dress up your table for an evening dinner party.

Designs | Michele Crawford

Project Specifications
Skill Level: Beginner
Table Runner: 56½" x 16½"
Placemat: 19" x 12½"
Napkin: 18½" x 18½"

Materials
¼ yard each tan print and light brick red print
⅜ yard each tan floral
½ yard cream tonal
¾ yard brick red leaf print
⅔ yard olive floral
1¼ yards floral stripe
(2) 14" x 21" placemat backings and (1) 19" x 60" runner backing
(2) 14" x 21" placemat battings and (1) 19" x 60" runner batting
(2) 3"-long green tassels for runner
⅓ yard green tasselled trim for napkin rings
All-purpose thread to match fabrics
Quilting thread

Note
The fabric listed will make one table runner, two placemats and two napkins.

Cutting
Cut one 19½" by fabric-width strip from floral stripe; subcut strip into two 19½" napkin squares.

Blooming Rose
12½" x 12½" Block
Make 5

Cut one 16½" by fabric-width strip from floral stripe; subcut strip into two 10½" x 16½" I rectangles and four 3¾" x 12½" G placemat borders. *Note: Make sure the strips cut from the floral stripe are identical in their printed stripe orientation.*

Cut one 4½" by fabric-width strip from olive floral; subcut strip into five 4½" A squares. Cut seven 2¼" by fabric-width strips for binding from olive floral.

Cut two 2½" by fabric-width strips from brick red leaf print; subcut strip into two 2½" x 36½" H runner borders.

Cut three 5¼" by fabric-width strips from brick red leaf print; subcut strips into (40) 2½" B rectangles.

Cut five 2½" by fabric-width strips from cream tonal; subcut strips into (80) 2½" C squares.

Cut two 4⅞" by fabric-width strips from tan floral; subcut strips into (10) 4⅞" squares. Cut each square in half on one diagonal to make 20 D triangles.

Cut two 2½" by fabric-width strips from the tan print; subcut strips into (20) 2½" E squares.

Cut two 2⅞" by fabric-width strips from light brick red print; subcut strips into (20) 2⅞" squares. Cut each square in half on one diagonal to make 40 F triangles.

Completing the Blocks

Mark a diagonal line on each C square. Place a marked C square right sides together to a B rectangle corner and stitch along the marked diagonal line. Trim seam to ¼" and press C to the right side. Repeat on opposite corner referring to Figure 1. Repeat to make 40 C-B units.

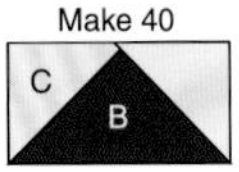

Make 40

Figure 1

Join two C-B units as shown in Figure 2; press seam in one direction. Repeat to make 20 joined units.

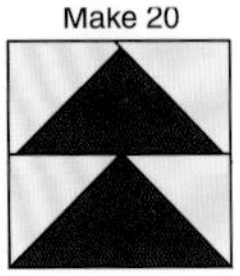

Make 20

Figure 2

Sew F triangles to two adjacent sides of an E square as shown in Figure 3; press seams toward E. Repeat to make 20 E-F units.

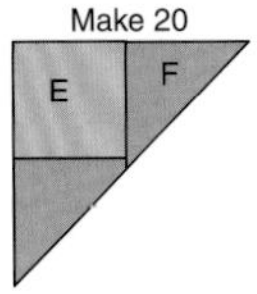

Make 20

Figure 3

Sew a E-F unit to D to complete a E-F-D unit as shown in Figure 4; press seam toward D. Repeat to make 20 E-F-D units.

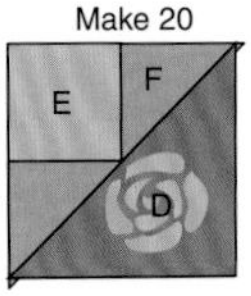

Make 20

Figure 4

Referring to Figure 5, arrange the units in rows and sew together; press seams in the direction of the arrows. Sew the rows together to complete each Blooming Rose block and press the seams toward the centre row. Repeat to complete five Blooming Rose blocks.

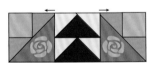

Figure 5

Blooming Roses

Completing the Placemats and Runner

To assemble the placemats, sew G borders to opposite short ends of one Blooming Rose block; press seams toward borders. Repeat on second block.

Sew the remaining three Blooming Rose blocks together to make the runner centre. Press the joining seams toward the centre block. Sew H borders to opposite long sides of runner centre; press seams toward borders.

Fold I in half along the 16½" side and mark center. Draw a line from each corner to the center mark and trim I rectangles along the lines as shown in Figure 6 for the runner points.

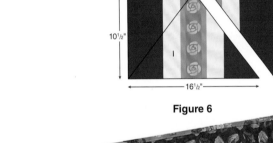

10½"

I

16½"

Figure 6

Referring to the Placement Diagram, sew a runner point to each end of the runner and press seams toward the points.

Layer placemat and runner with corresponding batting and backing; pin- or hand-baste the layers together.

Stitch in the ditch of all piecing seams. Do additional quilting in the blocks and borders if desired. *Note: No additional quilting was added to the sample placemats or runner.*

Machine-baste ⅛" from the outer edges of each quilted panel. Trim the excess batting and backing even with the quilt top.

Join binding strips on short ends to make one long strip. Press the seams open. Fold the binding strip in half lengthwise with wrong sides together and raw edges even; press.

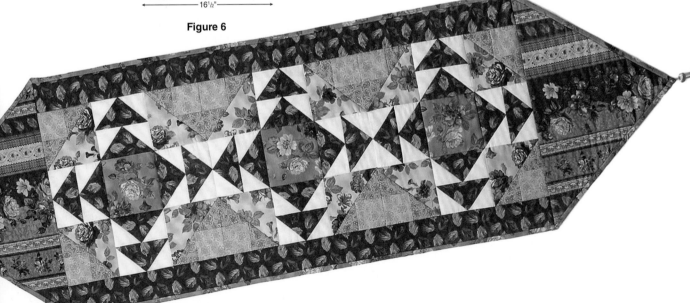

Beginning on the right side somewhere past the centre of one long edge of the runner, sew binding in place. Mitre the corners as you reach them and finish neatly at the place where the binding ends meet. Press the binding toward the seam allowance and wrap to the back of the quilt. Stitch in place. Bind the placemats in the same manner.

Sew a tassel to each point of the table runner.

Completing the Napkins

Make a narrow double hem on each napkin (or serge-finish with a rolled edge if you prefer).

For the napkin rings, cut two 5¾"-long pieces of tasselled trim. Fold each one in half and stitch the ends together a scant ¼" from the raw edges. Stitch again ⅛" from the first stitching. Turn right side out. Fold napkins and tuck each one into a napkin ring. ■

Blooming Roses Runner
Placement Diagram
56½" x 16½"

Blooming Roses Placemat
Placement Diagram
19" x 12½"

IT HITS THE SPOT RUNNER

Black and white is accented with red in this contemporary runner and napkin-ring set. Ribbon and yo-yos create the rings.

Designs | Chris Malone

Project Specifications

Skill Level: Beginner

Runner Size: Approximately 48" x 12"

Materials

Scrap white-with-black dot for napkin holders

⅛ yard each 7 black-with-white prints

⅛ yard each 3 white-with-black prints

⅔ yard red mottled

⅝ yard black-with-white print for napkins

Backing 54" x 18"

Batting 54" x 18"

All-purpose thread to match fabrics

Quilting thread

48" red 1½"-wide wire-edge ribbon

¼ yard lightweight fusible interfacing

Scrap heavyweight interfacing

2 red/black ⅞" buttons

Seam sealant

Note

The fabrics listed will make one table runner and two napkins and napkin holders.

Cutting

Cut black-with-white prints into approximately 22 assorted strips 12½" long and 2"–3" wide.

Prepare templates using patterns given on page 117; cut as directed on each piece, cutting interfacing to the size of the pattern and adding a ¼" seam allowance to fabric pieces when cutting.

Cut four 2¼" by fabric-width strips red mottled for binding.

Cut two 16" squares each black-with-white print and red mottled for napkins.

Runner

Completing the Runner

Arrange black-with-white print strips side by side, mixing widths and prints, until approximately 48" x 12". When satisfied with arrangement, join strips to make the runner base.

Centre and bond a fusible interfacing circle to the wrong side of a corresponding-sized fabric circle; repeat with all circles (except yo-yo circles).

Arrange the circles on the runner base, varying sizes and prints. When satisfied with arrangement, turn edges of fabric circles under edges of interfacing circles; hand- or machine-stitch in place.

Layer, quilt and bind referring to Getting Ready to Quilt on pages 14–17.

It Hits the Spot Runner

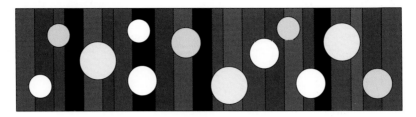

It Hits the Spot Runner
Placement Diagram
48" x 12"

Napkins

Completing the Napkins & Napkin Holders

Pin one 16" black-with-white print square right sides together with a red mottled square; sew all around, leaving a 3" opening along one edge. Clip corners and turn right side out; press. Repeat with second set of squares.

Fold in seam allowance of openings; press and slipstitch closed.

Topstitch ¼" from edges using black thread.

Apply seam sealant to the edges of each yo-yo circle.

Referring to Figure 1 and using a doubled thread, hand-sew a line of gathering stitches ⅛" from the edge of each circle.

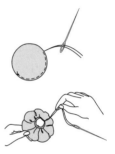

Figure 1

Place a yo-yo interfacing circle on the wrong side of the fabric and pull the stitches to gather tightly together in the centre.

Cut the ribbon into two 24" lengths; cut a V shape in each end of each piece.

Place one yo-yo on one ribbon length about 10" from one end and sew a button on the centre of the yo-yo through the ribbon. Repeat with second yo-yo and ribbon length.

Fold the napkin as desired and wrap ribbon around back and tie in a loose knot at the side to finish. ■

Large Circle
Cut 3 white-with-black prints
Cut 3 fusible interfacing
Add ¼" all around when cutting fabric circle

Yo-Yo Interfacing
Cut 2 heavyweight
interfacing

Yo-Yo Circle
Cut 2 white-with-black dot

Medium Circle
Cut 5 white-with-black prints
Cut 5 fusible interfacing
Add ¼" all around when cutting fabric circle

Small Circle
Cut 4 white-with-black prints
Cut 4 fusible interfacing
Add ¼" all around when cutting fabric circle

PLEASINGLY PAISLEY TABLE TOPPER

Stitch up this simple table topper with a colourful paisley print. Use it on your table to highlight your favourite centrepiece.

Design | Toby Lischko

Project Specifications
Skill Level: Beginner
Topper Size: 38" x 38"

Materials
⅜ yard gold tonal
⅝ yard green tonal
⅝ yard cream tonal
1 yard wine paisley
Backing 44" x 44"
Batting 44" x 44"
All-purpose thread to match fabrics
Quilting thread

Cutting
Cut two 6⅞" by fabric-width strips cream tonal; subcut strips into eight 6⅞" squares. Cut each square in half on one diagonal to make 16 A triangles.

Cut one 2⅞" by fabric-width strip each cream (D) and gold (F) tonals; subcut D strip into (12) 2⅞" squares and F strip into (14) 2⅞" squares. Cut each square in half on one diagonal to make 24 D and 28 F triangles.

Cut one 6⅞" by fabric-width strip each green (B) and gold (C) tonals; subcut B strip into six 6⅞" squares and C strip into two 6⅞" squares. Cut each square in half on one diagonal to make 12 B and four C triangles.

Cut two 2⅞" by fabric-width strips green tonal; subcut strips into (26) 2⅞" squares. Cut each square in half on one diagonal to make 52 E triangles.

Cut one 5⅞" by fabric-width strip each wine paisley (H) and green tonal (I); subcut each strip into two 5⅞" squares. Cut each square in half on one diagonal to make four each H and I triangles.

Cut four 5½" x 28½" G strips wine paisley.

Completing the Topper
Sew B to A along the diagonal to make an A-B unit as shown in Figure 1; press seam toward B. Repeat to make 12 A-B units.

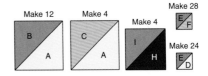

Figure 1

Repeat with A and C, H and I, D and E, and E and F to make four each A-C and H-I units, 24 D-E units and 28 E-F units, again referring to Figure 1.

Arrange the A-B and A-C units and join to make rows referring to Figure 2 (see page 120); press seams in adjacent rows in opposite directions. Join the rows to complete the pieced centre; press seams in one direction.

Pleasingly Paisley Table Topper

Make 2

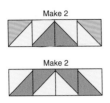

Make 2

Figure 2

Join six each E-F and D-E units to make a side strip as shown in Figure 3; press seams away from the centre of the strip. Repeat to make two side strips.

Make 2

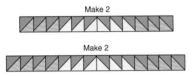

Make 2

Figure 3

Sew a side strip to opposite sides of the pieced centre; press seams away from the side strips.

Join six D-E units and eight E-F units to make the top strip, again referring to Figure 3; press seams away from the centre of the strip. Repeat to make the bottom strip.

Sew the pieced strips to the top and bottom of the pieced centre; press seams away from the strips.

Sew a G strip to opposite sides of the pieced centre; press seams toward the G strips.

Sew an H-I unit to each end of the remaining G strips as shown in Figure 4; press seams toward the G strips.

Figure 4

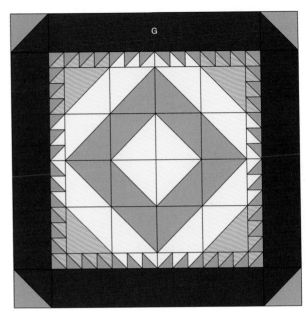

Pleasingly Paisley Table Topper
Placement Diagram
38" x 38"

Sew the G-H-I strips to the top and bottom of the pieced centre; press seams toward the G-H-I strips.

Figure 5

Complete the quilt referring to Getting Ready to Quilt on pages 14–17, except trim the batting even with the quilted top and trim the backing ¾" larger all around. Turn under the edge of the backing ¼"; press. Bring the folded backing to the front side, covering outer edge, and machine-stitch in place as shown in Figure 5 to finish. ■

TABLE GRACE

*A star block graces the centre
of this versatile table mat
that is ideal for afternoon tea.*

Design | Julie Weaver

Project Specifications
Skill Level: Beginner
Quilt Size: 24" x 24"
Block Size: 12" x 12"
Number of Blocks: 1

Materials
¼ yard cream tonal
¼ yard blue tonal
½ yard blue floral
⅔ yard light green tonal
Backing 30" x 30"
Batting 30" x 30"
All-purpose thread to match fabrics
Quilting thread

Cutting
Cut one 5¼" by fabric-width strip cream tonal; subcut strip into one 5¼" E square and eight 2½" F squares.

Cut one 5¼" by fabric-width strip blue tonal; subcut strip into one 5¼" C square, two 1½" x 12½" H rectangles and two 1½" x 14½" I rectangles.

Cut one 5¼" by fabric-width strip blue floral; subcut strip into two 5¼" D squares and four 2½" B squares.

Cut two 4" by fabric-width strips blue floral; subcut strip into two 15½" L rectangles and two 22½" M rectangles.

Cut one 4½" by fabric-width strip light green tonal; subcut strip into one 4½" A square and eight 2½" G squares.

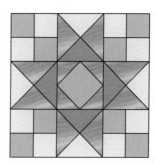

Four-Patch Star
12" x 12" Block
Make 1

Cut two 1" by fabric-width strips light green tonal; subcut strip into two 14½" J rectangles and two 15½" K rectangles.

Cut two 1½" x 22½" N strips, two 1½" x 24½" O strips and three 2½" by fabric-width strips for binding light green tonal.

Completing the Blocks
Draw a diagonal line from corner to corner on the wrong side of each B square.

Referring to Figure 1 (see page 122), place a B square right sides together on opposite corners of A and stitch on the marked lines; trim seam allowances to ¼" and press B to the right side.

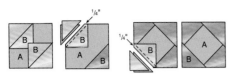

Figure 1   **Figure 2**

Repeat on the two remaining corners of A to complete the A-B centre unit as shown in Figure 2.

Cut each C, D and E square on both diagonals to make four each C and E triangles and eight D triangles.

Sew C to D and D to E as shown in Figure 3; press seams toward D. Repeat to make four each C-D and D-E units.

Make 4 each   Make 4

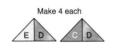

Figure 3   **Figure 4**

Sew a C-D unit to a D-E unit to complete a side unit as shown in Figure 4; press seam toward the C-D unit. Repeat to make four side units.

Sew F to G; press seam toward G. Repeat to make eight F-G units.

Join two F-G units as shown in Figure 5 to complete a corner unit; press seam in one direction. Repeat to make four corner units.

Make 4

Figure 5   **Figure 6**

Sew a side unit to opposite sides of the A-B centre unit to complete the centre row as shown in Figure 6; press seams toward the side units.

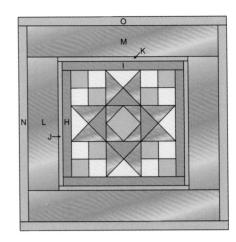

Table Grace
Placement Diagram
24" x 24"

Sew an F-G corner unit to opposite sides of each remaining side unit to make the top and bottom rows referring to Figure 7; press seams toward the side units.

Figure 7

Join the rows referring to the block drawing to complete the Four-Patch Star block; press seams in one direction.

Completing the Runner

Sew H strips to opposite sides and I strips to the top and bottom of the pieced block; press seams toward H and I strips.

Repeat with J through O strips referring to the Placement Diagram and pressing seams toward newly added strips as they are added to complete the pieced top.

Layer, quilt and bind referring to Getting Ready to Quilt on pages 14–17. ■

Table Grace

INDEX

INDEX

GENERAL INFORMATION

Metric Conversion Charts

Metric Conversions

yards	x	.9144	=	metres (m)
yards	x	91.44	=	centimetres (cm)
inches	x	2.54	=	centimetres (cm)
inches	x	25.40	=	millimetres (mm)
inches	x	.0254	=	metres (m)

centimetres	x	.3937	=	inches
metres	x	1.0936	=	yards

Standard Equivalents

⅛ inch	=	3.20 mm	=	0.32 cm
¼ inch	=	6.35 mm	=	0.635 cm
⅜ inch	=	9.50 mm	=	0.95 cm
½ inch	=	12.70 mm	=	1.27 cm
⅝ inch	=	15.90 mm	=	1.59 cm
¾ inch	=	19.10 mm	=	1.91 cm
⅞ inch	=	22.20 mm	=	2.22 cm
1 inch	=	25.40 mm	=	2.54 cm
⅛ yard	=	11.43 cm	=	0.11 m
¼ yard	=	22.86 cm	=	0.23 m
⅜ yard	=	34.29 cm	=	0.34 m
½ yard	=	45.72 cm	=	0.46 m
⅝ yard	=	57.15 cm	=	0.57 m
¾ yard	=	68.58 cm	=	0.69 m
⅞ yard	=	80.00 cm	=	0.80 m
1 yard	=	91.44 cm	=	0.91 m

1⅛ yards	=	102.87 cm	=	1.03 m
1¼ yards	=	114.30 cm	=	1.14 m
1⅜ yards	=	125.73 cm	=	1.26 m
1½ yards	=	137.16 cm	=	1.37 m
1⅝ yards	=	148.59 cm	=	1.49 m
1¾ yards	=	160.02 cm	=	1.60 m
1⅞ yards	=	171.44 cm	=	1.71 m
2 yards	=	182.88 cm	=	1.83 m
2⅛ yards	=	194.31 cm	=	1.94 m
2¼ yards	=	205.74 cm	=	2.06 m
2⅜ yards	=	217.17 cm	=	2.17 m
2½ yards	=	228.60 cm	=	2.29 m
2⅝ yards	=	240.03 cm	=	2.40 m
2¾ yards	=	251.46 cm	=	2.51 m
2⅞ yards	=	262.88 cm	=	2.63 m
3 yards	=	274.32 cm	=	2.74 m
3⅛ yards	=	285.75 cm	=	2.86 m
3¼ yards	=	297.18 cm	=	2.97 m
3⅜ yards	=	308.61 cm	=	3.09 m
3½ yards	=	320.04 cm	=	3.20 m
3⅝ yards	=	331.47 cm	=	3.31 m
3¾ yards	=	342.90 cm	=	3.43 m
3⅞ yards	=	354.32 cm	=	3.54 m
4 yards	=	365.76 cm	=	3.66 m
4⅛ yards	=	377.19 cm	=	3.77 m
4¼ yards	=	388.62 cm	=	3.89 m
4⅜ yards	=	400.05 cm	=	4.00 m
4½ yards	=	411.48 cm	=	4.11 m
4⅝ yards	=	422.91 cm	=	4.23 m
4¾ yards	=	434.34 cm	=	4.34 m
4⅞ yards	=	445.76 cm	=	4.46 m
5 yards	=	457.20 cm	=	4.57 m

GOT A PASSION FOR CRAFTING?

Each craft pattern book offers unique designs, easy-to-follow instructions, helpful how-to illustrations and full-colour photos—all for a very low price! Get creative and start a beautiful new project today for yourself or a loved one.

Crocheting Slippers
Crocheting Slippers provides 18 delightful patterns for cute and cozy slippers to keep the whole family's toes toasty. A handy stitch guide helps you put together these creative designs.

Crocheting Toys
In an age where so many things are mass-produced, the craft of crochet allows you to custom-create a toy or game for that special little one. These handcrafted toys will quickly become favourites and heartfelt reminders in years to come.

Quilting Pot Holders
Add flare to your kitchen with 45 unique designs for handy pot holders—you're sure to find something to suit any taste! *Quilting Pot Holders* includes full-colour photos of each project, useful instructions, templates and patterns.

Knitting for Dogs
Dogs are beloved members of our families, so of course we want to make them feel important with their own sweaters, beds and comfort toys. These fun designs will be a perfect match for your four-footed friend.

Sewing Aprons
Like to cook and love to sew? Just select one of our easy designs for fun and funky aprons that will keep your clothes clean while you're busy in the kitchen or the garden. Start sewing now, and stitch one for yourself or for a special friend!

Knitting Winter Accessories
Keep toasty warm when the cold winds blow with this great collection of knitted accessories. You'll find cozy hats, classy scarves, plus mittens and fingerless gloves. It's time to start knitting for a warm winter ahead.

We have a tasty lineup of cookbooks, with plenty more in the oven.

www.companyscoming.com

- Preview new titles
- Exclusive cookbook offers
- Find titles no longer in stores

Sign up for our FREE newsletter and receive kitchen-tested recipes every month!

Company's Coming